A Geographical History of the Qur'an

A GEOGRAPHICAL HISTORY OF THE QUR'AN

Syed Muzaffaruddin Nadwi

IBT

Islamic Book Trust
Kuala Lumpur

First published 1936
Sh Muhammad Ashraf,
Lahore, Pakistan

This revised edition 2009
Islamic Book Trust
607 Mutiara Majestic
Jalan Othman
46000 Petaling Jaya
Selangor, Malaysia
www.ibtbooks.com

Islamic Book Trust is affiliated to The Other Press.

Perpustakaan Negara Malaysia Cataloguing-in-Publication Data

Nadvi, Muzaffar Uddin, Syed, 1900-
A geographical history of the Qur'an / Syed Muzaffaruddin Nadwi.
Includes index
Bibliography: p. 145-146
ISBN 978-967-5062-17-9
ISBN 978-967-5062-18-6 (pbk.)
1. Koran--Geography. I. Title
939.4

Printed in Malaysia by
Academe Art and Printing Services, Kuala Lumpur.

Contents

Maps and Illustrations

Preface

Curiously enough, no serious attempt has been made to write a book on the geographical and historical backgrounds of the Qur'an with a view to proving the authenticity of the Qur'anic accounts and refuting the unjustified criticisms that have been levelled by the missionaries of non-Muslim faiths against the Qur'an. The only solitary exception is my learned teacher 'Allāmah Sayyid Sulaiman Nadwi's *Arḍ-ul-Qur'ān*, in Urdu, published in 1915, which is based on the most authoritative and reliable sources. For my part I had long cherished a desire to write a book on the subject in English for the English-speaking public. But after a careful consideration I came to the conclusion that I could not do better than assimilate the contents of that book and supplement them by extracts and quotations from other sources that have since come to light. As for example, the chapter on "Arabia and Colonialism" is almost entirely borrowed from the recently published Urdu book of Haji Mu'in-ud-Din Nadwi *The Existing States of Arabia*. This is the first volume of the book, and two other volumes will follow in due course.

The most difficult task in respect of ancient history is the fixing of periods and identification of names. Hence some principles should be borne in mind.

a. Fixation of time

It is essential from the view-point of modern history that periods of different peoples and tribes of Arabia should be ascertained. But the difficulty is that, so far as ancient history of Arabia is concerned, we have only three sources of information, and they are inadequate. These are:

1. The Old Testament, which is marked by its brevity and lack of details.
2. Arabian traditions, which do not mention dates.
3. Engraved tablets and monuments, which help us to know the dates of the deaths and conquests of some Arab monarchs.

Generally, to determine the period of any prehistoric nation we are to depend on its contemporary nations and individuals whose dates are known. Another method of ascertaining the dates is that we are to presume that four generations cover the period of one century. In this connection it must be noticed that the date of the existence of a nation may not necessarily be identical with the period of its rise to fame, for instance, the Banū Qaḥṭān flourished after Moses, but it does not follow that they had not come into existence earlier. Thousands of nations sprang up and lived in the world unknown for a long time, and then for some reason or other, some of these rose to power and glory. It is natural that first the individuals come into being, then they develop into a family, then into a society, and finally evolve into a nation.

b. Identification of names

To understand the home and nationality of an early people we have to find the connection between the names of historical persons and those of their places of residence, or between the languages of two peoples, or between the names of persons and those of gods. The similarity between the names of persons and those of their places enables us to ascertain the name of their countries, and the harmony between the languages of two nations points to their common origin. The first method of research is very helpful, particularly with regard to the ancient geography of the Semitic towns, because the Semitic races generally named towns and villages after their inhabitants. John Forster, who wrote *Historical Geography of Arabia* in the middle of the eighteenth century, has successfully utilised this principle, though in some places his conclusions are only hypothetical and open to objections.

c. Harmony in names and languages

Every nation has some peculiar forms of names. The Hindus, Muslims, Jews and Christians have all their own peculiar ways of naming the individuals of their community. Hence when we find that two nations have certain resemblances in names of men and place, we may presume that they belong to the same branch of the human race. Similarly, religious similarity and linguistic affinity between two nations bear testimony to their common origin.

The 'Ād, Thamūd, Saba, Jurham, etc., are very often assumed to be the names of persons, but in reality they are the names of tribes and peoples. For example, if we come to know that the first Arab kingdom was founded by Saba, it does not mean that any individual bearing the name of "Saba" founded the kingdom, but that the members of the Sabaean tribe did it (in Arabic generally the first part of genitive phrase is omitted, and so the word "Saba" stands for Banū Sabā, *i.e.*, descendants of Saba). Similarly, if we find that 'Ād lived for a thousand years, it means that the tribe of 'Ād lived for a thousand years and not any individual of that name.

Owing to the passage of time and variations in languages some names have assumed different forms in different languages, and consequently we may be misled into thinking that these names refer to different persons. If we compare the same names, as they are found in Arabic, Greek and other European languages, we shall be struck with the differences that have crept into them. Not to speak of the names of ancient peoples mentioned in the Qur'an, Muslim philosophers and thinkers who lived in comparatively recent times have been given different names in European languages, which do not bear any apparent resemblance to the original names, *e.g.*, Abū 'Alī Sīnā has been westernised into Avicenna, Ibn Rushd into Averroes, Ibn al-Haytham into Alhazem and Abū al-Qāsim into Albucasis. Similarly, the Hebrew "Yoktan" has been Hellenised into "Joktān" and Arabicised into "Qaḥṭān", and the Hebrew "Yerah" has been changed to "Jerah" in Greek and "Ya'rub" in Arabic. Such examples can easily be multiplied.

In spelling Oriental names I have tried to follow the system of transliteration approved by the Royal Asiatic Society. But I regret that owing to the inability of the Press this uniformity could not be retained in all cases, *e.g.*, "Z" has been used both for "ز" and "ظ" and "H" both for "ہ" and "ح".[1]

1. The present edition uses the transliteration system current in English books. — *Ed.*

In conclusion I must express my heartfelt thanks to my colleagues and friends for the assistance they have given me in compilation of this book, namely, Professor Abdul Baqi, MA, (Philosophy Department), Professor Abbas Ali Khan Bekhud, MA (Urdu Department) and Professor Md. Zuhur-ul Islam, MA (History Department) of the Islamia College, who went through the manuscript, gave me valuable suggestions and helped me in correcting proofs. My thanks are also due to Mr A. Quayyum Nu'mani, MA, Lecturer, St. James' College and Mr Shams-ul-Haque, MA, Lecturer, Islamia College for various kinds of help they have extended to me. Further I shall fail in my duty if I do not thank my former pupils, S.N. Hyder Rizvi, BA and S.M. Laiq who cooperated with me in preparing the Index. ❁

Syed Muzaffaruddin Nadwi
Lahore, 1936.

Introduction

The Arabs are a very ancient people, but their history is more or less uncertain. They are generally divided into two classes—pure and mixed. The former are descended from Joktān or Qaḥṭān (the son of Eber mentioned in Genesis X), while the latter trace their origin to Ishmael (Ismā'īl), a son of Abraham (Ibrāhīm) by Hagar, an Egyptian lady. The Arabs find references in the Old Testament as well as in classical literatures, which point to their antiquity and past glory. These references are further supplemented and confirmed by archaeological researches. Also in modern literatures of Europe, mention has been made of the perfumes and spices of Arabia, for example, Shakespeare says: "All the perfumes of Arabia will not sweeten this little hand", and Milton writes:

> As... off at sea northeast winds blow,
> Sabaean odours from the spicy shore,
> of Araby the blest.

Arabia rose to great importance about the beginning of the seventh century of the Christian era as the birthplace of a religion—Islam—which spread over a vast area of the then known world within a century of its inauguration, and which is now professed by more or less one-sixth of the human race, and also as the place of revelation of a book—Qur'an—which, in the words of Washington Irving, "contains pure, elevated and benignant precepts", which, in the words of Steingass, "is one of the grandest books ever written", which, in the words of Goethe, "attracts, astounds and enforces our reverence", and which, in the words of Hirshfeld, "is unapproachable as regards convincing power, eloquence and even composition".

The Qur'an was originally intended to be a guide to Arabia and through Arabia to the whole world. The Arabs had long been immersed in polytheism and idol-worship, besides being addicted to drinking, gambling and other immoral acts. When Prophet Muḥammad (ṣ) first announced that his mission was to lead the people to the right path, to purge them of their vices and to cure them of their ills, the entire country rose against him. For so stubborn a people the sudden revelation of a book of the size of the Qur'an could not be suitable. The Qur'an was, therefore, revealed piecemeal and by instalments, and its revelation covered the whole period of Muḥammad's prophethood. It took the Qur'an some thirteen years to prepare the ground and clear up the atmosphere of the country, and it was only in the latter half of the period of the Prophet's mission that the verses of the Qur'an began to be appreciated by the bulk of the people. The Qur'an is, in the words of Johnson, "a Prophet's cry, semitic to the core, yet of a meaning so universal and so timely that all the voices of the ages take it up, willingly or unwillingly, and it echoes over chosen hearts to world-conquest, then gathering itself into a reconstructing force that all the creative light of Greece and Asia might penetrate the heavy gloom of Christian Europe when Christianity was but the Queen of Night".

Some Orientalists, who have translated the Qur'an or written anything concerning it, have asserted that the verses and chapters of the Qur'an remained scattered and disjointed during the lifetime of the Holy Prophet, and that they were collected after his death on the authority of the verbal evidences of the Companions, and hence its genuineness is liable to question. This assertion only serves to betray the ignorance of those who make it. It is an untruth to say that the verses and chapters of the Qur'an were collected after the Prophet's death, for there is strong historical evidence to prove that all verses of the Qur'an were collected and all the sūrahs (chapters) named by the direct instruction of the Prophet himself.

The process of collection was that whenever the verses were revealed the Prophet directed his scribes, the chief of whom was Zayd bin Thābit, to place verses of similar nature together in one sūrah (chapter) and himself gave the name to each sūrah. Sometimes it so happened that verses of two sūrahs were revealed simultaneously, and the Prophet got them recorded separately so as to avoid confusion. Thus towards the close of the Prophet's life all the verses had been arranged and sūrahs named. What was done by Caliph Abū Bakr was to arrange these sūrahs in the order suggested by the Holy Prophet, and no more. The third Caliph, 'Uthmān, simply issued an official copy of the Qur'an (which was an exact copy of the one prepared by Abū Bakr), gave it publicity and forbade the use of other copies (which differed from official one only in the method of reading), so that different readings might not lead to differences of doctrine, such as have actually occurred in other religions. Thus there were three stages in the assembling together of the verses of the Qur'an in a volume. The first was Collection, and that was made during the lifetime of the

Prophet himself; the second was Compilation (in the shape of a book), and that was effected by Caliph Abū Bakr at the request of 'Umar, and the third stage was Enforcement or Publicity, and that was given by Caliph 'Uthmān.

I quote but a few out of many pieces of reliable evidence available in support of the facts I have set out above.

1. Ḥudhayfah, a Companion of the Prophet, narrates that the Prophet recited certain verses of the sūrah al-Baqarah (Chap. 1), of Āl 'Imrān (Chap. 3) and of al-Nisā' (Chap. 4) in some of his prayers.

2. It is recorded in *Ṣaḥīḥ al-Bukhārī*, the most authentic book of Ḥadīth, that the Prophet recited certain verses of al-A'rāf (Chap. 7) in prayers.

3. Several traditions in the various books of Ḥadīth unmistakably show that the Companions knew the names of the different sūrahs which the Prophet recited, partially or wholly, in his prayers from time to time.

4. Ḥākim writes in his book Mustadrik that the first collection of the Qur'an was made during the lifetime of the Prophet himself.

5. The same traditionist has narrated the following in the name of Zayd bin Thābit: "We used to collect the verses of the Qur'an in the presence of the Prophet, copying them from various pieces of paper." (This statement is authentic and altogether reliable, satisfying all that conditions of Bukhārī and Muslim).

6. "The copying of the Qur'an was not nothing new. The Prophet himself ordered the copying of it."

The above testimony is confirmed by verses of the Qur'an itself. A few of such verses are given here:

> *Nay, surely it (the Qur'an) is an admonition. So let him read it who pleases. (It is written) in honoured books (which are) exalted and purified, in the hands of scribes, noble and virtuous.* (80:11-16)

According to Imām Rāzī these scribes refer to the Companions of the Prophet, but according to some commentators to those who committed the Qur'an to memory.

Again says the Qur'an:

> *Most surely it is an honoured Qur'an, in a book that is protected; none shall touch it, save the purified ones.* (56:77-79)

> *Surely on Us (devolves) the collecting of it [the Qur'an] and the reciting of it. Therefore when We have recited it, follow its recitation. Again, on Us (devolves) the explaining of it.* (75:17-19)

> *Surely We have revealed it [the Qur'an] with truth, and surely We will protect it.* (15:9)

> *A Prophet from Allah recites pure books, containing reasonable instructions.* (98:2-3)

The verses quoted above show clearly that the Qur'an did not, in the Prophet's time, consist only in scattered and disconnected fragments, but that it was a well-arranged and jealously protected piece of work.

It may be added here that all the pre-Islamic poems of Arabia which have come down to us are recognised by the

Orientalists in general as correct, though they, too, have been compiled on the verbal evidences of the Arabs. How is it, then, that the Qur'an, which was committed to memory by a considerable number of the Companions, and was recorded by others, cannot be recognised as genuine by the same Orientalists?[2]

The Qur'an being the last revealed book takes stock of the previous religions and makes references to some important peoples and countries of the world. These references are testified to by quotations from the Bible and classical authors and corroborated by archaeological researches. It is gratifying to note that several European Orientalists have taken the trouble to explore Arabia, trace the relics of her glorious past, discover her monuments and decipher their inscriptions. Their explorations and researches have confirmed the Qur'anic description of peoples and countries.

For the verification of the geographical and historical references in the Qur'an we mainly depend upon: (1) Islamic literature; (2) Jewish literature; (3) classical literatures; (4) archaeological discoveries. We discuss below these four sources of information in detail.

Islamic literature

During the time of the Prophet, Muslims did not care to study the political or historical condition of the races mentioned in the Qur'an chiefly because they were at that time too much engrossed in religious discussions to think of anything else. But when Islam passed beyond the confines of Arabia, subsequent Muslims thought it necessary to acquaint themselves with the

---

2. See my article "The Qur'an and the Orientalists", *The Islamic Review*, Lahore, April 1935.

past history of Arabia and her people. For this purpose the following materials were employed:

1. *The Qur'an*, which briefly touches on various peoples of Arabia and some other lands.

2. *The Traditions,* mentioned in the Commentaries of the Qur'an, *i.e.* commentators in explanation of the geographical references found in the Qur'an have quoted some traditions of the Prophet and his Companions. Such traditions are, however, very few.

3. *The Old Testament*, *i.e.*, the Muslims acquired some information regarding the geographical references in the Qur'an from the Old Testament which makes mention of a number of tribes of Arabia as well as other parts of the world. It should, however, be noted here that the Old Testament in its present form does not, in several cases, give us correct and accurate information, and some of the events mentioned therein are no better than fictions.

4. *The Arabs' ancestral traditions and legends*, *i.e.*, the Arabs generally excelled in retaining the names of their ancestors and their achievements. When the Muslims developed the art of writing, such traditions were embodied in books. This source of information is, generally speaking, open to objections, but there can be no doubt about the authenticity of those traditions and evidences which have been unanimously agreed upon by the Arabs, *e.g.*, the stay of Ishmael at Makkah, the foundation of the Ka'bah, the genealogy of the Quraysh up to 'Adnān, etc.

5. *Poems and proverbs of the Arabs, i.e.*, Arab writers boastfully described historical facts about the achievements of their ancestors and also of other peoples. A close study of such poems and proverbs can give some clue to the geographical and political conditions of some tribes of Arabia.

Muslim scholars have, however, classified Islamic literature on the subject as follows:

1. *Commentaries of the Qur'an.* Some of the Commentators of the Qur'an have explained the geographical references of the Holy Book by quoting facts and evidences from other sources.

2. *History of Arabia.* A number of books were compiled by early Muslim scholars on the history of Arabia and her people. The first such book was written during the reign of Caliph Mu'āwiyah (40-60 AH).

3. *Geography of Arabia.* The Muslims began to write on the geography of Arabia at a time when they knew nothing of the Greek word *geography.* Though they did not write separate books on the "Land of the Qur'an", they in the course of geographical investigations discussed many lands and tribes mentioned in the Qur'an. On this subject two sorts of books were compiled by the Arabs; (*i*) those which dealt with the geography of Arabia only, and (*ii*) those which treated several countries including Arabia.

4. *Genealogy.* The Arabs are perhaps the only people who developed genealogy into a distinct branch of learning. We find that even a child of Arabia in early times could reproduce from his memory the names and attainments of his forefathers. During the pre-

Islamic as well as post-Islamic periods many persons excelled in genealogy. When the compilation of books was taken in hand by Muslims, they wrote a number of books on that subject also.

Jewish literature

From the time of Moses till the advent of Islam in the seventh century CE, a number of books came into existence, some of which were revealed and others the results of human efforts. As the primary theme of the Qur'an and Jewish books was similar, a large number of facts and events were common between them.

Jewish literature is composed of the following works:

1. *Torah,* which was revealed to Moses. It consists of the following five books (collectively known as Pentateuch): (a) *Genesis,* which deals with the creation of the universe and also gives a short account of Adam, Eve, Noah, Abraham, Joshua, Ishmael, Jacob and Joseph; (b) *Exodus,* which gives an account of Moses and Pharaoh and of the going out of the Israelites from Egypt (1491 BC); (c) *Leviticus,* which contains laws and dogmas of the faith and mentions what is lawful and what is unlawful; (d) *Numbers,* which gives the number of the Israelites at the time of their exodus from Egypt, and also mentions wars of Moses and some laws of his religion; (e) *Deuteronomy,* which contains a repetition of the discourses of Moses and of the laws given in Exodus.

2. *Nebhīm* (the Prophets), divided into two groups: (a) the "Former Prophets", such as Joshua, Samuel and others; (b) the "Latter Prophets", such as Isaiah, Ezekiel, and others.

3. *Kethubim* (the Writings), consisting of Psalms, Proverbs, Songs of Solomon, Esther, Daniel, etc.
4. *Targum*, the Aramaic translation and commentary of the Torah and Nebhīm.
5. *Midrash*, the traditions of the Jews.
6. *Talmud*, the jurisprudence of the Jews.

The classical literatures

Several Greek and Roman historians, geographers and adventurers have mentioned in their books some of those countries and tribes which have been referred to in the Qur'an. Some of these writers were contemporaries of those tribes and peoples and, therefore, their information may be taken as reliable.

The following classical authors are noteworthy:

1. *Herodotus* (484-425 BC). He wrote a history of Greece and Persia, briefly touching on Egypt, Africa and Arabia. Greece had never been directly connected with Arabia, but as the Arabs generally sided with the Persians in their wars with the Greeks, the author thought it necessary to make mention of the Arabs also. His book has been translated into Arabic. The knowledge of Herodotus regarding Arabia was, however, very limited. He thought that Arabia was the last southern country beyond which there was no human habitation. Further, he was entirely unaware of the Persian Gulf which divided Arabia from Persia.

   A century after Herodotus, Alexander the Great led an invasion into Egypt and Persia in 332-331 BC, and his soldiers had an opportunity to know the Persian Gulf and the borders of Arabia. He had a wish to conquer the yet unconquered land of Arabia, but owing to his sudden death in 323 BC, it remained unfulfilled. Nevertheless, the Greeks owing to their diplomatic relations with Egypt and Persia, frequently came in contact with Arab merchants of Alexandria and the Persian Gulf. Naturally, therefore, the Greeks began to know more and more about the Arabs.

2. *Eratosthenes* (276-194 BC). He was superintendent of the Alexandria Library during the Greek period and compiled a general geography of the world. This book is now lost, but some portions of it were incorporated by Strabo (d. 24 BC) in his book. Fortunately, the chapter on Arabia is extant.

3. *Diodorus* (born in Sicily in 80 BC). He wrote a book in which he gave an account of Arabia, the Nabataean empire and the Holy Ka'bah. But a great portion of the book is lost.

4. *Strabo* (63-24 BC). His work on geography, while describing the expedition led by the Romans into Arabia under General Aelius Gallus, touches on the Nabataeans and makes a passing reference to Negrana (Najrān) and Mariaba (Ma'rib), the two well-known towns of Arabia.

5. *Pliny* (23-79 CE). He has left us a book entitled *Natural History*, in which he has described the eastern coasts of Arabia and also the expedition which the Romans led into Arabia with a view to making a discovery of the coasts of the East.

6. *Ptolemy*. He was an astronomer and geographer of Alexandria in the second century CE. This was the period when the Roman Empire was at the height of its glory. Ptolemy prepared a map of the world and then compiled a geographical book in amplification of it. This book was first translated into Arabic by Ya'qūb al-Kindī, but as the translation was not sufficiently intelligible, Thābit bin Qurrah produced a new translation of it in the ninth century CE.[3] The original map of Ptolemy is lost, but the book is extant.

   Ptolemy himself never visited Arabia, but he frequently met Arab merchants at Alexandria and from them he acquired some information regarding that country. On the basis of that information he prepared the geography of Arabia. He divided Arabia into three natural divisions: (a) Arabia Felix; (b) Arabia Petra; (c) Arabia Deserta.

   Ptolemy has given an elaborate description of all famous tribes, towns, villages, mountains, coasts and commercial routes of Arabia. But their names have since changed so radically that it is wellnigh impossible to understand most of them. The well-known author Bunbury has rejected this book as based on imagination and fiction. But the German Orientalist, Sprenger, whose book *Ancient Geography of Arabia* was published in 1875, has scrutinised the information contained in Ptolemy's book, and after verifying it from the works of the Arab geographers has characterised the same to be reliable.

3. Ibn al-Nadīm, *Kitāb al-Fihrist*, p. 268.

Muslim geographers, such as Mas'ūdī and Yāqūt Ḥamawī, have, however, complained in their works that Ptolemy's book is most unintelligible, that the Arab tribes, who generally led unsettled and nomadic lives, have been misunderstood and misinterpreted by Ptolemy, and that his book cannot be taken as a reliable and authentic source of information on the subject.

In addition to the Greek and Roman authors there was a Jewish author in this period who deserves mention. His name was Josephus Flavius who lived at Alexandria during the first century of the Christian era. He has left a number of books in Greek and Latin on the history and religion of the Jews. These books have been translated into English. His works *History of the Jewish War*, *Antiquities of the Jews* and *Philosophy of the Jews*, which contain much valuable evidence bearing upon Biblical history, are regarded very important, partially because their author was the only Jewish historian of the ancient time and partially because he flourished during the period when the famous Alexandria Library was still in existence.[4]

Archaeological discoveries

There are many monuments in different parts of Arabia which contain inscriptions and engravings, and from these the archaeological experts have arrived at some interesting conclusions. These inscriptions are mostly found in Ḥimyaritic, Sabaean, Aramaic and Nabataean characters. During the latter part of the Umayyad rule and the earlier part of the Abbasids, these inscriptions were deciphered. Some scholars of the time knew foreign languages and characters, for instance, Dhū al-Nūn al-Miṣrī, who flourished in the

4. The Alexandria Library was founded by, and grew quickly during the time of, the first Ptolemy, Demetrius Phabreus. When Julius Caesar besieged Alexandria the major portion of the library was set on fire.

second century AH, could easily decipher the old Egyptian inscriptions. Some important discoveries made by Muslim explorers are given below:

1. Hamdānī, the well-known geographer, has enumerated the famous remains of Arabia in his book *al-Iklil* (The Crown) and briefly described them in his book *Ṣifātu Jazīrat-il-'Arab.*[5] The fort "Nā'iṭ" was built on the top of a mountain by the King of Yemen fifteen hundred years before Islam. It contained an inscription which was later deciphered by Wahab bin Manba' who was a Companion of the Companions of the Prophet. It is translated as follows: "This edifice was erected at a time when we had our corns from Egypt." Wahab says that after calculation he found that the fort had been built exactly sixteen hundred years before.[6]

2. During the reign of Mu'āwiyah (40-60 H.) 'Abd al-Raḥmān, Governor of Egypt, discovered an inscription in a ruined fort of Ḥaḍramawt, named *Ḥiṣn al-Ghurāb.* That inscription has been rendered into English by John Forster as follows:

   And we hunted the game, by land, with ropes and reeds:
   And we drew forth the fishes from the depths of the sea.
   Kings reigned over us, far removed from baseness,
   And vehement against the people of perfidy and fraud.
   They sanctioned for us, from the religion of Hūd (Heber)

---

5. This book has been edited by D.H. Müller.

6. Yāqūt has referred to this fort in his book *Mu'jam al-Buldān*. Poet Amru al-Qays also refers to it in his verse which says: He it is who can muster round thousands of men of the tribe of Banū Asad from the height of the fort Na'it."

right laws,
And we believed in miracles, the resurrection, and the resurrection of the dead by breath of God.
When enemies descended upon our soil to invade us,
We went forth together, with straight and dusky spears.[7]

The Mission which the East Indian Company had despatched to Yemen in 1834 got the above inscription in the Ḥimyaritic character. John Forster (1812-76) is of opinion that the inscription belongs to the 'Ād and is one of the oldest inscriptions of Arabia dating as far back as 1800 years BC.

3. During the lifetime of the famous historian Kalbī a certain person of the tribe of Dhū al-Kalā' found a throne at Yemen with a corpse on it and a golden shield decked with rubies lying by its side. On the throne the following inscription was found:

In the name of God who is the Lord of the Ḥimyarites I am Ḥassān, son of 'Amar Nafil.[8]

4. Hammād Rāwī's nephew found an arrow of the 'Ād on the top of a mountain with some verses inscribed on it, which can be translated thus:

Shall we be able, before our death, to go back to the houses situated in Dhū al-Lawa? These are the towns wherein we lived and which we loved, and this was at the time when these towns were real towns and their inhabitants were real inhabitants.[9]

---

7. J. Forster, *Historical Geography of Arabia*, Vol. II pp. 90-93, which copies the inscription from Nuwayrī's book, *Masaliku'l-Absar.*

8. *Mu'jam al-Buldān.*

9. *Mu'jam al-Buldān.*

5. Ibn Hishām writes that once in Yemen a certain tomb was found open due to flood and a corpse of a woman, with seven laces of pearls on her neck and rings decked with gems on her fingers, was taken out of the tomb. A slab was also found with an inscription which has been translated by John Forster as follows:

> In thy name, O God, the God of Himyar,
> I, Tajāh, the daughter of Dhū Shefār sent my steward to Joseph,
> And he delaying to return to me, I sent my handmaid
> With a measure of silver to bring me back a measure of flour:
> And not being able to procure it, I sent herewith a measure of gold,
> And not being able to procure it, I sent herewith a measure of pearls,
> And not being able to procure it, I commanded them to be ground;
> And finding no profit in them, I am shut up here.
> Whosoever may hear of me, let them commiserate me.
> And should any woman adorn herself with an ornament from my ornaments, may she die by no other than my death.[10]

The above inscription, which relates to the period of Joseph, fully confirms the Qur'anic description of the famine which severely ravaged different countries in those days. This inscription further shows that some

10. J. Forster, *op. cit.*, Vol. II, pp. 102, 103.

Arabs knew the art of writing in a very early age and that the Ḥimyarites took Allah as their Lord.

Hamdānī (d. 334 H), who excelled in archaeological researches, has described all such inscriptions in the eighth book of his great work *al-Iklīl*. Besides him, Muqaddasī, Yāqūt, Nuwayrī, Qazwīnī, etc., have mentioned such discoveries and inscriptions in their books.

Now to come to the discoveries made by the West. European scholars and adventurers were originally interested in discovering those places which were mentioned in the Old Testament. As most of these places are situated in or near Arabia they had to direct their expeditions into Babylon, Egypt, Palestine, etc.

Niebuhr was the first European traveller and adventurer who proceeded to Arabia. He began his journey in 1761 and went alone to Yemen. When war broke out between Muḥammad 'Alī Pāshā (Khedive[11] of Egypt) and the King of Nejd, Europe sided with Egypt. Thus European adventurers had an easy access to different parts of Arabia. It may not be out of place to mention here that most of them were actuated more by political aspirations than by their thirst of knowledge. The researches and discoveries made by these European travellers are detailed in a book compiled by D.G. Hogarth. A summary of this book appears in *Encyclopaedia Britannica* (Vol. II, Art. "Arabia") which is quoted below.

The article under reference describes: (1) What parts the Europeans have been able to visit; (2) What monuments and inscriptions they have been able to discover.

11. Persian for Lord, a title first used by Muḥammad 'Alī Pāshā for governor or monarch of Egypt and Sudan.

THE FIRST PART

Modern Exploration in Yemen

The region most thoroughly explored is Yemen, in the south-west corner of the peninsula, where the labours of a succession of travellers from Niebuhr in 1761 to E. Glaser and R. Manzoni in 1887 have led to a fairly complete knowledge of all that part of the province west of the capital Sana; while in 1902-1904 the operations of the Anglo-Turkish boundary commission permitted the execution of a systematic topographical survey of the British protectorate from the Red Sea to the Wadi Bana, 30 m. east of Aden, North of Yemen up to the Hejaz border the only authority is that of E.F. Jomard's map, published in 1839, based on the information given by the French Officers employed with Ibrahim Pasha's army in 'Asīr from 1824 to 1827, and of J. Halevy in Najrān. On the south coast expeditions have penetrated but a short distance, the most notable exceptions being those of L. Hirsch and J.T. Bent in 1887 to the Ḥaḍramawt Valley. S.B. Miles, J.R. Wellsted, and S.M. Zwemer have explored Oman in the extreme east; but the interior south of a line drawn from Taif to El-Katr on the Persian Gulf is still virgin ground. In northern Arabia the Syrian Desert and the great Nafud (Nefud) have been crossed by several travellers, though a large area remains unexplored in the north-east between Kasim and the gulf. In the centre, the journeys of W. Palgrave, C. Doughty, W. Blunt and C. Huber have done much to elucidate the main physical features of the country. Lastly, in the north-west the Sinai Peninsula has been thoroughly explored, and the list of travellers who have visited the Holy Cities and traversed the main pilgrim routes through Hejaz is a fairly long one, though, owing to the difficulties peculiar to that region, the hydrography of southern Hejaz is still incompletely known.

The story of modern exploration begins with the despatch of C. Niebuhr's mission by the Danish Government in 1761. After a year spent in Egypt and the Sinai Peninsula the party reached Jidda towards the end of 1762, and after a short stay sailed on to Lohaia in the north of Yemen, the exploration of which formed the principal object of the expedition; thence, travelling through the Tehama or lowlands, Niebuhr and his companions visited the towns of Bet-el-fakih, Zubed and Mokha, then the great port for the coffee trade of Yemen. Continuing eastward they crossed the mountainous region and reached the highlands of Yemen at Uden, a small town and the centre of a district celebrated for its coffee. Thence proceeding eastwards to higher altitudes where coffee plantations give way to fields of wheat and barley, they reached the town of Jibla situated among a group of mountains exceeding 10,000 ft. above sea-level: and turning southwards to Taiz descended again to the Tehama *via* Hes and Zubed to Mokha. The mission, reduced in numbers by the death of its archaeologist, Von Haven, again visited Taiz in June, 1763, where after some delay permission was obtained to visit Sana, the capital of the province and the residence of the ruling sovereign or Imam. The route lay by Jibla, passing the foot of the lofty Jebel Sorak, where in spite of illness, Forskal, the botanist of the party, was able to make a last excursion; a few days after he died at Yarim. The mission continued its march, passing Dharnar, the seat of a University of the Zedi sect, then frequented by 500 students. Thence four marches, generally over a stormy plateau dominated by bare, sterile mountains, brought them to Sana, where they received a cordial welcome from the Imam, el-Mehdi Abbas. The aspect of the city must have been nearly the same as at present: Niebuhr describes the enceinte flanked by towers, the citadel at the foot of J. Nukum which rises 1,000 ft. above the valley, the fortress and palace of the Imams now replaced by the Turkish military hospital, the suburb of Bir-el-Azab with its scattered houses and gardens, the Jews' quarter and the village of Rauda, a few miles to the north in a fertile, irrigated plain which Niebhur compares to that of Damascus. After a stay of ten days at Sana the mission set out again for Mokha, travelling by what is now the main route from the capital to Hodeda through the rich coffee-bearing district of J. Haraz, and thence southward to Mokha, where they embarked for India. During the next year three other members of the party died leaving Niebuhr the sole survivor. Returning to Arabia a year later he visited Oman and the shores of the Persian Gulf and travelling from Basrah through Syria and Palestine he reached Denmark in 1764 after four years' absence. The period was perhaps specially favourable for a scientific mission of the sort. The outburst of fanaticism which convulsed Arabia twenty years later had not then reached Yemen, and Europeans, as such, were not exposed to any special danger. The travellers were thus able to move freely and to pursue their scientific enquiries without hindrance from either people or ruler. The results published in 1772 gave for the first time a comprehensive description not only of Yemen but of all Arabia; while the parts actually visited by Niebuhr were described with a fulness and accuracy of detail which left little or nothing for his successor to discover.

Exploration in Jauf, Ma'rib and 'Asīr

C.G. Ehrenberg and W.F. Hemprich in 1825 visited the Tehama and the islands off the coast, and in 1836 P.E. Botta made an important journey in southern Yemen with a view to botanical research, but the next advance in geographical knowledge in south Arabia was due to the French Officers, M.O. Tamisier, Chedufau and Mary, belonging to the Egyptian army in Asir; another Frenchman, L. Arnaud, formerly in the Egyptian service, was the first to visit the southern Jauf and to report on the rock-cut inscriptions and ruins of Marib, though it was not till 1869 that a competent archaeologist, J. Halevy, was able to carry out any complete exploration there. Starting from Sana, Halevy went northeastward to El-Madid, a town of 5,000 inhabitants and the capital of the small district of Nihm; thence crossing a plateau, where he saw the ruins of numerous crenellated towers, he reached the village of Mijzar at the foot of J. Yam, on the borders of Jauf, a vast sandy plain, extending eastwards to El-Jail and El-Hazam, where Halevy made his most important discoveries of Sabaean inscriptions; here he explored Ma'īn the ancient capital of the Minaeans, Kamna on the banks of the W. Kharid, the ancient Caminacum, and Kharibat-el-Beda, the Nesca of Pliny, where the Sabaean army was defeated by the Romans under Aelius Gallus in 24 BC. From El-Jail Halevy travelled northward passing the Oasis of Khas and skirting the great desert reached the fertile district of Najrān, where he found a colony of Jews with whom he spent several weeks in the Oasis of Makhlaf. An hour's march to the east he discovered at the village of Madinatul Mahud the ruins of the Nagra metropolis of Ptolemy. In June, 1870, he at last reached the goal of journey, Ma'rib; here he explored the ruins of Madinat an Nahas (so called from its numerous inscriptions engraved on brass plates) and two hours to the east he found the famous dam constructed by the Ḥimyarites across the W. Shibwan, on which the water supply of their capital depended.

One other explorer has since visited Ma'rib, the Austrian archaeologist E. Glaser (1855-1908), who achieved more for science in Yemen than any traveller since Niebuhr. Under Turkish protection he visited the territory of the Hashid and Bakel tribes northeast of Sana and though their hostile attitude compelled him to return after reaching their first important town, Khamr, he had time to reconnoitre the plateau lying between the two great Kharrid and Hirran, formerly covered with Ḥimyaritic towns and villages and to trace the course of these wadis to their junction at El-Ish in the Dhu Husen country and thence onward to the Jauf.

In 1889 he succeeded, again under Turkish escort, in reaching Ma'rib, where he obtained during a stay of 30 days, a large number of new Ḥimyaritic inscriptions. He was unable however to proceed farther east than his predecessors and the problem of the Jauf drainage and its possible connection with the upper part of the Ḥaḍramawt valley still remains unsolved.

Exploration in Ḥaḍramawt

The earliest attempt to penetrate into the interior from the south coast was made in 1835 when Lieuts. C. Cruttenden and J.R. Wellsted of the "Palinurus" employed on the marine survey of the Arabian coast, visited the ruins of Nabk (el-Hajar) in the W. Mefat. The Ḥimyaritic inscriptions found there and at Husn Ghurab near Mukalla were the first records discovered of ancient Arabian civilization of Ḥaḍramawt. Neither of these officers was able to follow up their discoveries, but in 1843 Adolph von Wrede landed at Mukalla and adopting the character of a pilgrim to the shrine of the prophet Hūd, made his way northward across the high plateau into the W. Duwan, one of the main southern tributaries of the Ḥaḍramawt valley, and pushed on to the edge of the great southern desert; on his return to the W. Duwan his disguise was detected and he was obliged to return to Mukalla. Though he did not actually enter the main Ḥaḍramawt valley, which lay to the east of his track, his journey established the existence of this populous and fertile district which had been reported to the officers of the "Palinurus" as lying between the coast range and the great desert to the north. This was at last visited in 1893 by L. Hirsch under the protection of the Sultan of Mukalla, the head of the Kaiti family, and practically ruler of all Ḥaḍramawt, with the exception of the towns of Saiyun and Tarim, which belong to the Kathiri tribe.

Starting like von Wrede from Mukalla, Hirsch first visited the W. Duwan and found ancient ruins and inscriptions near the village of Hajren; thence he proceeded northeastward to Hauta in the main valley, where he was hospitably received by the Kaiti Sultan, and sent on to his deputy at Shibam. Here he procured a Kathiri escort and pushed on through Saiyun to Tarim, the former capital. After a very brief stay, however, he was compelled by the hostility of the people to return in haste to Shibam; from which he travelled by the W. Bin Ali and W. Adim back to Mukalla. J. Theodore Bent and his wife followed in the same track a few months later with a well-equipped party, including a surveyor, Imam Sharif, lent by the Indian Government, who made a very valuable survey of the country passed through. Both parties visited many sites where Ḥimyaritic remains and inscriptions were found, but the hostile attitude of the natives, more particularly of the Seyyids, the religious hierarchy of Ḥaḍramawt, prevented any adequate examination, and much of the archaeological interest undoubtedly remains for future travellers to discover.

Exploration in Oman

In Oman, where the conditions are more favourable, explorers have penetrated only a short distance from the coast. Niebuhr did not go inland from Muscat; the operations by a British Indian Force on the pirate coast in 1810 gave no opportunities for visiting the interior and it was not till 1835 that J.R. Wellsted, who had already tried to penetrate into Ḥaḍramawt from south, landed at Muscat with the idea of reaching it from the northeast. Sailing thence to Sur near Ras-el-Had, he travelled southward through the country of the Banibu Ali to the borders of the desert, then turning northwest up the Wadi Betha through a fertile, well-watered country, running up to the southern slopes of J. Akhdar, inhabited by a friendly people who seem to have welcomed him everywhere, he visited Ibra, Semed and Nizwa at the southern foot of the mountains. Owing to the disturbed state of the country due to the presence of raiding parties from Nejd, Wellsted was unable to carry out his original intention of exploring the country to the west, and after an excursion along the Batina coast to Sohar he returned to India.

In 1876 Colonel S.B. Miles, who had already done much to advance geographical interests in the South Arabia, continued Wellsted's work in Oman. Starting from Sohar on the Batina coast he crossed the dividing range into the Dhahira and reached Birema, one of its principal oases. His investigations show that the Dhahira contains many settlements with an industrious agricultural population and that the unexplored tract extending 250 m. west to the peninsula of El-Katr is a desolate gravelly steppe, shelving gradually down to the salt marshes which border the shores of the gulf.

Exploration in Hejaz

Leaving southern Arabia, we now come to the centre and north. The first explorer to enter the sacred Hejaz with a definite scientific object was the Spaniard, Badiay Iablich, who under the name of 'Alī Bey and claiming to be the last representative of the Abbasid Caliphs, arrived at Jidda in 1807, and performed the pilgrimage to Mecca. Besides giving to the world the first accurate description of the holy city and the Haj ceremonies, he was the first to fix the position of Mecca by astronomical observations and to describe the physical character of its surroundings. But the true pioneer of exploration in Hejaz was J.L. Burckhardt, who had already won a reputation as the discoverer of Petra, and whose experience of travel in Arab lands and knowledge of Arab life qualified him to pass as a Moslem, even in the headquarters of Islam. Burckhardt landed in Jidda in July, 1914, when Mehemet Ali had already driven the Wahhabi invaders out of Hejaz and was preparing for his farther advance against their stronghold in Nejd. He first visited Taif at the invitation of the Pasha, thence he proceeded to Mecca, where he spent three months studying every detail of the topography of the holy places, and going through all the ceremonies incumbent on a Moslem pilgrim. In January, 1815 he travelled to Medina by the western coast route, and arrived there safely, but broken in health by the hardships of the journey. His illness did not, however, prevent his seeing and recording every thing of interest in Medina with the same care as at Mecca, though it compelled him to cut short the further journey he had proposed to himself and to return by Yambu and the sea of Cairo, where he died only two years later.

His striking successor, Sir Richard Burton, covered nearly the same ground thirty-eight years afterwards. He, too, travelling as a Moslem pilgrim, noted the whole ritual of the pilgrimage with the same keen observation as Burckhardt, and while amplifying somewhat the latter's description of Medina, confirms the accuracy of his work there and at Mecca in almost every detail. Burton's topographical descriptions are fuller, and his march to Mecca from Medina by the eastern route led him over ground not traversed by any other explorer in Hejaz: this route leads at first southeast from Medina, and then south across the lava beds of the Harra, keeping throughout its length on the high plateau which forms the border land between Hejaz and Nejd. His original intention had been after visiting Mecca to find his way across the peninsula to Oman, but the time at his disposal (as an Indian Officer on leave) was insufficient for so extended a journey; and his further contributions to Arabian geography were not made until twenty-five years later, when he was deputed by the Egyptian government to examine the reported gold deposits of Midina. Traces of ancient workings were found in several places, but the ores did not contain gold in paying quantities. Interesting archaeological discoveries were made, and a valuable topographical survey was carried out, covering the whole Midian coast from the head of the gulf of Akaba to the mouth of "Wadi Hamd" and including both the Tehama range and the Hisma valley behind it, while the importance of the "Wadi Hamd" and the extent of the area drained by its tributaries was for the first time brought to light.

Exploration in Nejd

Burckhardt had hoped in 1815 that the advance of the Egyptian expedition would have given him the opportunity to see something of Nejd, but he had already left Arabia before the overthrow of the Wahhabi power by Ibrahim Pasha had opened Nejd to travellers from Hejaz, and though several European officers accompanied the expedition, none of them left any record of his experience. It is, however, to the Egyptian conquest that the first visit of a British traveller to Nejd is due. The Indian Government, wishing to enter into relation with Ibrahim Pasha, as *de facto* ruler of Nejd and El-Hasa, with a view to putting down piracy in the Persian gulf, which was seriously affecting Indian trade, sent a small mission under Captain G.F. Sadlier to congratulate the Pasha on the success of the Egyptian arms, and no doubt with the ulterior object of obtaining a first-hand report on the real situation. On his arrival at Hofuf, Sadlier found that Ibrahim had already left Deraiya, but still hoping to intercept before quitting Nejd, he followed up the retreating Egyptians through Yemama, and Wushm to Ras in Kasim, where he caught up the main body of Ibrahim's army, though the Pasha himself had gone on to Medina. Sadlier hesitated about going farther, but he was unable to obtain a safe conduct to Basrah, or to return by the way he had come, and was compelled reluctantly to accompany the army to Medina. Here he at last met Ibrahim, but though courteously received, the interview had no results, and Sadlier soon after left for Yambu, whence he embarked for Jidda, and after another fruitless attempt to treat with Ibrahim, sailed for India. If the political results of the mission were nil, the value to geographical science was immense; for though no geographer himself, Sadlier's route across Arabia made it possible for the first time to locate the principal places in something like their proper relative positions; incidentally, too, it showed the practicability of a regular troops crossing the deserts of Nejd even in the months of July and August.

Sadlier's route had left Jebel Shammar to one side; his successor G.A. Wallin was to make that the objective of his journey. Commissioned by Mohemet Ali to inform him about the situation in Nejd brought about by the rising power of Abdullah Ibn Rashid, Wallin left Cairo in 1845, and crossing the Pilgrim road at Ma'ān, pushed on across the Syrian Desert to the Wadi Srihan and the Jauf Oasis, where he halted during the hot summer months. From the wells of Shakik he crossed the waterless Nafud in four days to Jubba, and after a halt there in the nomad camps he moved on to Hail, already a thriving town and the capital of the Shammar State, whose limits included all northern Arabia from Kasim to the Syrian border. After a stay in Hail, where he had even opportunity of observing the character of the country and its inhabitants and the hospitality and patriarchal, if sometimes stern, justice, of its chief, he travelled on to Medina and Mecca and returned thence to Cairo to report to his patron. Early in 1848 he again returned to Arabia, avoiding the long desert journey by landing at Muwela, thence striking inland to Tebuk on the pilgrim road, and re-entering Shammar territory at the oasis of Tema, he again visited Hail; and after spending a month there travelled northwards to Kerbela and Bagdad.

Palgrave's journey to Nejd

The effects of the Egyptian invasion had passed away, and central Arabia had settled down again under its native rulers when W.G. Palgrave made his adventurous journey through Nejd, and published the remarkable narrative which has taken its place as the classic of Arabian exploration. Like Burton he was once an officer in the Indian Army but for some time before his journey he had been connected with Jesuit mission in Syria. By training and temperament he was better qualified to appreciate and describe the social life of the people than their physical surroundings, and if the results of his great journey are disappointing to the geographer, his account of the society of the Oasia towns, and of the remarkable men who were then ruling in Hail and Riad, must always possess an absorbing interest as a portrait of Arab life in its fresh development.

Following Wallin's route across the desert by Ma'ān and Jauf, Palgrave and his companion, a Syrian Christian, reached Hail in July, 1862, here they were hospitably entertained by the Amir Talal, nephew of the founder of the Ibn Rashid dynasty, and after some stay passed on with his countenance through Kasim to southern Nejd. Palgrave says little of the desert part of the journey or of its Bedouin inhabitants but much of the fertility of the Oases, and of the civility of the townsmen; and like other travellers in Nejd he speaks in enthusiasm of its bright, exhilarating climate at Riad. Fesal, who had been in power since the Egyptian retirement, was still reigning; and the religious tyranny of Wahhabism prevailed, in marked contrast to the liberal regime of Talal in Jebel Shammar. Still, Palgrave and his companions, though known as Christians, spent nearly two months in the capital without molestation, making short excursions in the neighbourhood, the most important of which was to El Kharfa in Aflaj, the most southernly district of Nejd. Leaving Riad, they passed through Yemama, and across a strip of the sandy desert to El-Hasa where Palgrave found himself in more congenial surroundings. Finally, a voyage to the Oman coast and a brief stay there brought his adventures in Arabia to a successful ending.

Doughty

Charles Doughty, the next Englishman to visit northern Arabia, though he covered little new ground, saw more of the desert life and has described it more minutely and faithfully than any other explorer. Travelling down from Damascus in 1875 with the Haj caravan he stopped at El-Hajr, one of the pilgrim stations, with the intention of awaiting the return of the caravan and in the meantime of exploring the rock-cut tombs of Medain Salih and El-Ala. Having successfully completed his investigations and sent copies of inscriptions and drawings of the tombs to Renan in Paris, he determined to push on farther into the desert. Under the protection of a Sheikh of the Fukara Bedouin he wandered over the whole of the borderland between Hejaz and Nejd. Visiting Tener, where among other ancient remains he discovered the famous inscribed stone, afterwards acquired by Huber for the Louvre. Next summer he went on to Hail and thence back to Khaibar, where the Negro Governor and townsmen, less tolerant that his former Bedouin host, ill-treated him and even threatened his life. Returning to Hail in the absence of the Amir, he was expelled by the governor, he succeeded, however, in finding protection at Aneza, where he spent several months, and eventually after many hardships and perils found his way to the coast at Jidda.

Three years later Mr Wilfrid and Lady Anne Blunt made their expedition to J. Shammar. In their previous travels in Syria they had gained the confidence and friendship of a young Sheikh, whose family, though long settled at Tadmur, came originally from Nejd and who was anxious to renew the connexion with his kinsmen by seeking a bride among them. In his company the Blunts set out from Damascus, and travelled across the Syrian Desert by the Wadi Sirman to Jauf. Here the Sheikh found some of his relations and the matrimonial alliance was soon arranged. But though the object of the journey had been attained, the Blunts were anxious to visit Hail and make the acquaintance of the Amir Ibn Rashid, of whose might and generosity they daily heard from their hosts in Jauf. The long stretch of waterless desert between Jauf and J. Shammar was crossed without difficulty, and the party was welcomed by the Amir and hospitably entertained from a month after which they travelled northwards in company with the Persian Pilgrim caravan returning to Kerbela and Bagdad.

Huber

In 1883 the French traveller C. Huber accompanied by the archaeologist, J. Euting, followed the same route from Damascus to Hail. The narrative of the last named forms a valuable supplement to that published by the Blunts, and together with Doughty's furnishes as complete a picture as could be wished for of the social and political life of J. Shammar, and of the general nature of the country. Huber's Journal, published after his death from his original notes, contains a mass of topographical and archaeological detail of the greatest scientific value; his routes and observation form, in fact, the first and only scientific data for the construction of the map of northern Arabia. To archaeology also his services were of equal importance, for, besides copying numerous inscriptions in the district between Hail and Tema, he succeeded in gaining possession of the since famous Tema stone, which ranks with the Moabite stone among the most valuable of semitic inscriptions. From Hail, Huber followed nearly in Daughty's track to Aneza and thence across Central Nejd to Mecca and Jidda, where he despatched his notes and copies of inscriptions. A month later in July, 1884, he was murdered by his guides a few marches north of Jidda, on his way back to Hail.

One other traveller visited Hail during the lifetime of the Amir Mohammad—Baron E. Nolde—who arrived there in 1893, not long after the Amir had by his victory over the combined forces of Riad and Kasim brought the whole of Nejd under his dominion. Nolde crossed the Nafud to Haiyania by a more direct track than that from Shakik to Jubba. The Amir was away from his capital settling the affairs of his newly acquired territory; Nolde, therefore, after a short halt at Hail journeyed on to Ibn Rashid's camp somewhere in the neighbourhood of Shakra. Here he was on new ground, but unfortunately he gives little or no description of his route thither or of his journey northwards by the Persian Pilgrim Road, already traversed by Huber in 1881. His narrative thus, while containing much of general interest on the climate and on the animal life of Northern Arabia, its horses and camels in particular, adds little to those of his predecessors as regards topographical detail.

General results of exploration

If the journeys detailed above be traced on the maps they will be found to cover the northern half of the peninsula above the line Mecca-Hofuf, with a network of routes, which, though sometimes separated by wide intervals, are still close enough to ensure that no important geographical feature can have been overlooked, specially in a country whose general character varies so little over wide areas. In the southern half, on the other hand, except in Najrān and Jauf, no European traveller has penetrated 100 m. in a direct line from the coast. The vast extent of the Dahnā', or great southern desert, covering perhaps 250,000 sq. m., accounts for about a third of this area, but some of the most favoured districts in Arabia—'Asīr and northern Yemen—remain unexplored, and the hydrography of the Dawasir Basin offers some interesting problems, while a great field remains for the archaeologist in the seat of the old Sabaean Kingdom from Jaul to the Ḥaḍramawt Valley.

The Second Part

Antiquities

Arabia cannot be said to be "destitute of antiquities", but the material for the study of these is still very incomplete. The difficulties in the way of travelling in Arabia with a view to scientific investigation are such that little or nothing is being done, and the systematic work which has given such good results in Egypt, Palestine and Babylonia-Assyria is unknown in Arabia. Yet the passing notes of travellers from the time of Carsten Niebuhr show that antiquities are to be found.

Prehistoric Remains

Since prehistoric remains must be studied where they are found, the difficulty in the way of exploration makes itself severely felt. That such remains exist seems clear from the casual remarks of travellers. Thus Palgrave (*Central and Eastern Arabia*, Vol. I, Ch. 6) speaks of part of a circle of roughly shaped stones taken from the adjacent limestone mountains in the Nejd. Eight or nine of these stones still exist, some of them 15 ft. high. Two of them, 10 to 12 ft. apart, still bear their horizontal lintel. They are all without ornament. Palgrave compares them with the remains at Stonehenge and Karnek Doughty (*Arabia Dererta*, Vol. II), travelling in northwest Arabia saw stones of granite in a row and "flagstones set edgewise" (though he does not regard these as religious), also "round heaps", perhaps barrows and "dry-built round chambers", which may be ancient tombs. J.T. Bent (*Southern Arabia*, pp. 24 ff.) explored one of several mounds in Bahrain. It proved to be a tomb and the remains in it are said to be Phoenician.

Castles and Walls

In the south of Arabia where an advanced civilization existed for centuries before the Christian era, the ruins of castles and city walls are still in existence and have been mentioned, though not examined carefully, by several travellers. In Yemen and Ḥaḍramawt especially these ruins abound, and in some cases inscriptions seem to be still *in Situ*. Great Castles are often mentioned in early Arabian literature. One in the neighbourhood of Sana was described as one of the wonders of the world by Qazwini (*Athār-ul-Bilād*, p. 33 ed. Wustenfeld, Gottingen, 1847, *cf. Journal of the German Oriental Society*, Vol. VII. pp. 472, 476, and for other castles, Vol. X, pp. 20 ff.), the ruins of the city of Ma'rib, the old Sabaean capital, have been visited by Arnaud, Halevy and Glaser, but call for further description, as Arnaud confined himself to a description of the dike (see below) while Halevy and Glaser were interested chiefly in the inscriptions.

Wells and Dikes

From the earliest times the conservation of water has been one of the serious cares of the Arabs. All over the country wells are to be found, and the masonry of some of them undoubtedly ancient. Inscriptions are still found of these in the south. The famous well Zemzem at Makkah is said to belong to the early times, when the Eastern traffic passed from the south to the northwest of Arabia through the Hejaz, and to have been rediscovered shortly before the time of Mahomet. Among the most famous remains of Ma'rib are those of a great dike reminding one of the restored tanks familiar to visitors at Aden. These remains were first described by Arnaud (*Journal Asiatique*, January, 1874, with plan). The importance was afterwards emphasized by Glaser's publication of two long inscriptions concerning their restoration in the 5th and 6th centuries AD (Zwei Inschriften uber den Dammbruch von Ma'rib, in the *Mitteilungen-der Vordersasiatischen Gesellschaft*, Berlin, 1897). Another dike about 150 yds. long was seen by W.B. Harris at Hirran in Yemen. Above it was a series of three tanks (*A Journey through Yemen*, p. 279, London, 1893).

Stones and Bronzes

The 19th century has brought to the museums of Europe (especially to London, Paris, Berlin and Vienna) a number of inscriptions in the languages of Minaei and Saba and a few in those of Ḥaḍramawt and Katabania (Qattabania). These inscriptions are generally on limestone or marble or on tablets of bronze and vary from a few inches to some feet in length and height. In some cases the originals have been brought to Europe, in other cases only squeezes of the inscription. The characters employed are apparently derived from the Phoenician (*cf. Lidzbarski's Ephemeris*, Vol. I, pp. 109 ff.). The languages employed have been the subject of much study (*cf.* F. Hommel's *Subarabische Chrestomathie*, Munich, 1893) but the archaeological value of these remains has not been so fully treated. Very many of them are native inscriptions and contain little more than the names of gods and princes or private men. A few are historical, but being (with few and late exceptions) undated, have given rise to much controversy among scholars. Their range seems to be from about 800 BC (or 1500 BC according to E. Glaser) to the 6th century AD. Few are still *in situ* the majority having been taken from their original position and built into houses, mosques or wells of more recent date. Among these remains are altars, and bases for statues of gods or for golden images of animals dedicated to gods. The earlier stones are devoid of ornamentation, but the later stones and bronzes are sometimes ornamented with designs of leaves, flowers, ox-heads, men and women. Some bear figures of the conventionalized sacred trees with worshippers, similar to Babylonian designs. Besides these there are grave-stones, stelae with human heads, fragments of limestone, architectural designs as well as bronze castings of camels, horses, mice, serpents, etc. (*cf.* D.H. Müller's *Südarabische Alterthumer in Kunsthistorischen*, Museum, Vienna, 1899, with plates).

Seals, Weights and Coins

The Vienna Museum possesses a small number of seals and gems. The seals are inscribed with Sabaean writing and are of bronze, copper, silver and stone. The gems of onyx, carnelian and agate are later and bear various figures and in some cases Arabic inscriptions. One or two weights are also in existence. A number of coins have been brought to the British Museum from Aden, Sana and Ma'rib. Others were purchased by G. Schlumberger in Constantinople; others have been brought to Europe by Glaser and are now in the Vienna Museum. These are imitations of Greek models, while the inscriptions are in Sabaean characters (*cf.* B.V. Head, in the *Numismatic Chronicle*, 1878, pp. 273-284, G. Schlumberger, *Le Tresor de Sana*, Paris, 1880, D.H. Müller, *op. cit.*, pp. 65 ff. and Plates).

A number of books have recently been written on Arabia, which have considerably added to our knowledge of that country, particularly H. St. J.B. Philby's *The Empty Quarter and Arabia of the Wahhabis*, Amīn Rihani's *Around the Coasts of Arabia* and *Arabian Peak and Desert*, and Haji Mu'in-ud-Din Nadvī *The Existing States of Arabia*. The first-named book is very important as it describes the great South Desert of Arabia (Rub 'al-Khālī), unknown even to the Arabs and explored by its author (Mr Philby) for the first time in history. The journey described in this book is one of the boldest feats in the history of Arabian exploration, and I cannot resist the temptation of quoting some passages from its introductory chapter for the information of the readers.

When all is said and done, the Empty Quarter would seem to be far from justifying the lurid colours in which it has been painted by some European travellers, and in which it is always painted by the Arabs of settled tracts who have never been within view of it, though the crossing of it is an adventure not to be lightly undertaken by the uninitiated (*The Heart of Arabia*, Vol. II p. 217). None had crossed Arabia before me except one—Captain G.F. Sadlier, my predecessor by hundred years.

Dr Hogarth on the other hand was the right-hand man of the British Government on all matters of Arabian import. Director of the Wartime Arab Bureau at Cairo, he was the acknowledged and pre-eminent authority on Arabian affairs. And as far back as 1904 he had, under the title of the "Penetration of Arabia", published an exhaustive and inspiring summary of all that had been done in the field of Arabian Exploration from the days of Nearchus and Aelius Gallus up to the beginning of the twentieth century. The gaps he had noted in our knowledge of Arabia were still for the most part gaps after the lapse of fourteen years. And one of them was perhaps the largest blank on the map of the earth outside the Polar regions. He was content to contemplate its vast silence without encouraging rash adventurers to their doom. The end of science could be served as well in other ways. If oxygen could surmount the summity of Everest, the aeroplane or even the motor car could surely expose the emptiness of the Empty Quarter in all good time. But he would perhaps scarcely have credited a forecast that within fourteen years more the Rub 'al-Khālī would have yielded up its secrets, not once, but twice to ordinary travellers equipped with no means of locomotion that has not been at the service of explorers since the beginning of time. Yet no one desired more intensely to know the exact nature of that great emptiness, and the suppressed twinkle of his cautious cynicism was more than a spur of inspiration. More than anything I regret that he himself had passed beyond the veil before the veil was drawn from an earthly mystery of whose significance he would have been the ideal interpreter.

From pleasant weeks of closest contact with Dr Hogarth at Jidda and in Egypt I passed that year back into Arabia and down into its southern depths round the great Wadi of the Dawasir, where I had to turn back regretfully on June 6th, 1918, having to rest content with what had been achieved and the hope of satisfying some day the insatiable craving within me to penetrate the recesses of that Empty Quarter, whose northern boundary I had now skirted along its whole length from East to West, from Hasa to the Wadi (*The Heart of Arabia*, Vol. II p. 216).

I had then unveiled a part of the unknown south, but only enough to whet my appetite for more. From my companions—and particularly from one Jabir ibn Faraj of the Great Murra tribe—I had heard of mysterious ruins in the heart of the further sands and of a great block of iron as large as a camel. And through their spectacles I had a glimpse of the Empty Quarter. But that was all, and I knew that an opportunity for further investigation of those mysteries would not soon occur—if ever. "I hope someday," I wrote, "that another more fortunate than I may be able to test the veracity of my informers" (*ibid.*, p. 222). That hope was partly fulfilled in the exploits of Major Cheesman (1924) and Mr Thomas (1931), and I could scarcely expect that between them they might have left me anything to do when my own turn should come in due course.

Meanwhile though unsuccessful, I had not been idle. The vicissitudes of life and work had carried me out of Arabia for ever, but the magnet held the needle. And to Arabia I went back in the Autumn of 1934 to try a throw with fate. To that effort and its consequences I sacrificed everything—the security of an orthodox career and the rest of it.

PART I
Geography of Arabia

1
Introduction

There are three versions regarding Arabia being so named:

1. The Arabic word *'Arab* is derived from *I'rāb* which means "to express one's mind". As the Arabs regarded themselves eloquent speakers, they gave themselves the name of Arab (and their country the name of Arabia) and the rest that of 'Ajam (*i.e.*, dumb).

2. Some genealogical experts say that the first inhabitant of the country now known as Arabia was Ya'rub, the son of Qaḥṭān, and forefather of the Arabs of Yemen, and hence the whole country was known as Arabia and its inhabitants as Arabs after him. But this theory is against historical evidence as well as common analogy. Neither was Ya'rub the first inhabitant of Arabia nor can the world *'Arab* be derived from Ya'rub under any linguistic rule. Moreover, the home of Ya'rub was Yemen and so Yemen or south Arabia should have been named Arabia first and the rest afterwards, but we know

that in the first instance the name was applied to north Arabia and not to south Arabia.

3. Geographers generally say, and rightly so, that the first name of the country was *'Arabah* which, in the course of time, became 'Arabia, and afterwards the people were named Arabs after their country.

In all Semitic languages the word *'Arabah* means desert (in Hebrew it means a field or a forest, and in Arabic it relates to the nomadic life), and as the country of Arabia is largely a desert or forest without water or pasture, specially that portion which extends from Ḥijāz to Syria and Sinai, the country was named as 'Arabah and the people gradually were known as Arabs. The verses of Arabian poets also testify to this view.[12]

In the Qur'an the word *'Arab* has never been used for the country of Arabia. The Qur'an has characterised the residence of Prophet Ishmael as an "uncultivated land". It is, therefore, obvious that God has only described the natural condition of Arabia—the same idea that is conveyed by the word 'Arabah". As during the time of Ishmael his place of residence had no name, it was given the name of an "uncultivated land". In the Old Testament the word *Midbar* has been used for Ishmael's home, and this word also means a desert or a barren land, which exactly corresponds to the Qur'anic description of the same.

In the Old Testament the word "Horeb" has been repeatedly used in the sense of a particular tract of the land of Arabia, *i.e.*, that piece of land which extends from Ḥijāz to

12. Ibn Munfidh Thawrī, a pre-Islamic poet of Arabia, says: "We have got a camel which disgrace has not touched, and its place of shelter is at 'Arabah, Qarn and Abṭaḥā." Abū Sufyān Kalbī, a post-Islamic poet of Arabia, says: "Our father (Ishmael) was the Prophet of God and the son of His friend (Abraham). He settled us at 'Arabah. How excellent is our place of settlement!"

Syria and Sinai (Deuteronemy, i. 6.). For the whole country of Arabia generally the term "East" has been used in the Bible,[13] and occasionally the term "South" also,[14] because Arabia is situated on the south-eastern side of Palestine.

Arabia was first mentioned during the time of Solomon in 1000 BC (I Kings, x. 15), and afterwards frequently in Hebrew, Greek and Roman books of history. The cuneiform inscriptions of Assyria of 800 BC contain the word "Aribi" in the sense of Arabia.[15] Before the advent of Islam the term *'Arab* applied to the whole country of Arabia extending from Yemen to Syria. ❁

13. Genesis, Judges and Kings.
14. Matthew and Genesis.
15. Roger, *History of Babylon and Assuria*, Vol. II. p. 127.

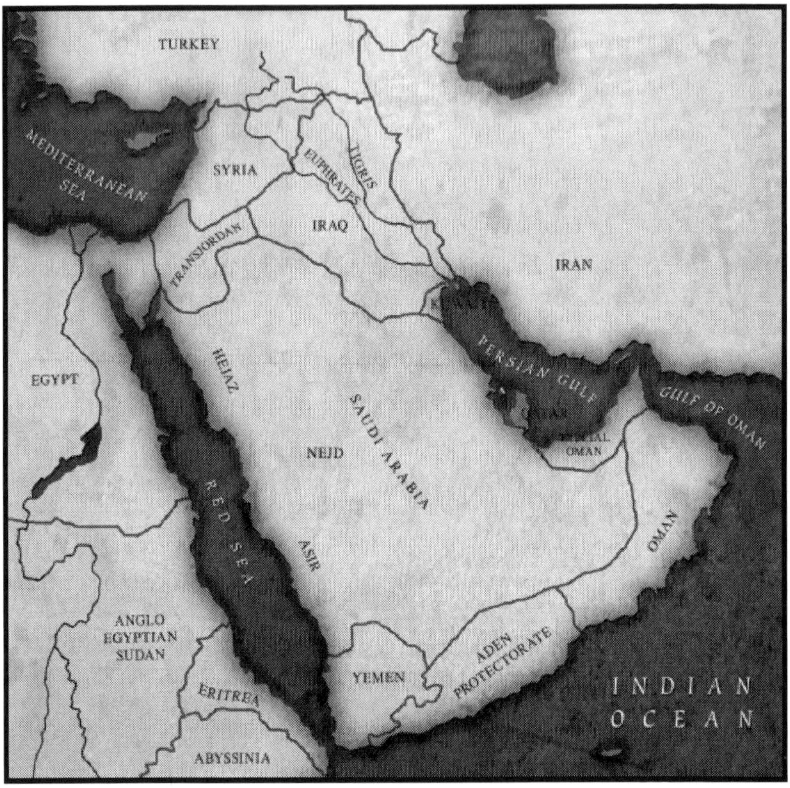

Arabia during the colonial era

2

Arabia in the Old Testament (2500–500 BC)

Name of Arabia

The first name of Arabia was "The Land of the East" (Genesis, ii) and the second name was "The Land of the South."[16] Both the names were applied by Prophet Abraham (Genesis, xxv. 6). In north Arabia, from time immemorial, the following tribes had been living: the Edomites, the Moabites, the Ammonites, the Amorites, the Midianites, and the Amalekites. Though the Hebrews knew something of their neighbouring country, *viz.*, north Arabia, they could not give any definite name of that place. Hence they generally referred to every piece of land after the tribes inhabiting it, *eg.*, "The Land of Edom", "The Land of Moab", "The Land of Amalek", and so forth. During the time of Moses, when the Israelites passed from Egypt to a certain far-off land in north Arabia across the Red Sea, they saw that the whole place was a large tract of desert, and so they gave that land the name of Horeb (Arabia) (Deuteronomy, 1-6), while other parts of Arabia continued to be named after their inhabitants as before.

16. W.L. Bevan, *Ancient Geography* (1871), p. 8.

During the time of Solomon the Hebrews were at the height of their glory. We are told in the Bible that "King Solomon made a navy of ships in Eziongeber, which is beside Eloth, on the shore of the Red Sea, in the land of Edom... And they came to Ophir, and fetched from thence gold, four hundred and twenty talents, and brought it to king Solomon." (1 Kings, ix. 26-28). The Hebrews subjugated all northern and some southern districts (*eg.*, Saba) of Arabia. Thus they were acquainted with the natural boundaries of Arabia. They, therefore, applied the term "Arabia" to the whole country (1 Kings, x. 15).

Divisions of Arabia

The Hebrews had no knowledge of the geography of Arabia. For a long time they knew only of north Arabia which comprised Ḥijāz, Sinai, Arabian Syria, Arabian Iraq, Bahrain and coasts of the Persian Gulf. They divided north Arabia into two parts—the land of the east and the land of the west. The former included the towns that lay to the east of Canaan, the coastal places of the Persian Gulf, Bahrain, and Arabian Iraq; while the latter comprised Sinai, Ḥijāz, the Syrian Desert of Arabia and a portion of Nejd situated on the south of Canaan. A number of tribes lived in these eastern and southern parts of north Arabia, and each tract of land was named after its inhabitants.

The towns of Arabia

Of all the towns of Arabia, "Mesha" and "Sepher", which marked the extreme boundaries of the land of the Qaḥṭānids, have received the first mention in the Old Testament (Genesis, v. 30). "Sepher" has been understood for Ẓafār situated in Yemen, but there is no town in Arabia of the name of Mesha. Rev. Bevan is of the opinion that Mesha is a substitute for

"Muza", a town situated on the Arabian coast near the mouth of the Red Sea.[17] A town of the name of "Moosa", which finds mention in the map of Ptolemy[18] and which is situated on the coast of Yemen, may also have been intended by "Mesha". This word may also stand for "Makkah", as one of the sons of Prophet Ishmael is mentioned in the Old Testament under the name of Masa, and it is quite possible that this town was founded by or named after him. G. Sale, the English translator of the Qur'an, favours this view.[19]

The Old Testament has mentioned several towns that were included in the land of Edom. Their situations, however, have not been given in the Scripture; but as they were parts of the land of Edom, they must be traced in north-west Arabia. "Bozrah" of the Old Testament is certainly the same town that is known among the Arabs as "Busra", and "Teman" of the Bible may, perhaps, be identical with "Tīmā'ī"—a well-known town near Busra. The position of the other ancient capitals of the kings of Edom—Dinhabad Avith, Rehoboth and Pan (Gen. xxxvi. 32, 35, 37, 39)— cannot be identified.[20]

The Old Testament mentions a place under the name of "Hazor" in connection with Kedar, son of Ishmael (Jer. xlix. 28), but as far as we know there is no town in Arabia of that name, and hence this word should not be taken as the name of any particular town, but only in the sense of a permanent residence. (The word "Hazor" literally means a permanent habitation as opposed to "Bādiyah" which means a temporary one).

---

17. *ibid.*, p. 9.
18. Hogarth.
19. Sale, *Translation of the Qur'an,* "Introduction".
20. Bevan, *op. cit.*, p. 9.

Another famous town is mentioned in the Old Testament under the name of Shiloh (1 Kings, xiv. 4), which was included in the country of Edom. The word "Shiloh" means stone, which corresponds to the Arabic *al-Ḥajar* and Greek *Petra*. Until the Greek period it had been a magnificent city, and its ruins are still visible near Syria on the north of Arabia. The port "Eloth" near the gulf of 'Aqabah was a part of the kingdom of Edom (2 Kings, viii. 17) which was later conquered by the peoples of David and Solomon and made headquarters of the naval power of the Israelites. The vessels of Solomon used to pass from Eloth to another port named Ophir situated in south Arabia (2 Kings, viii. 18). The latter port, a commercial centre, has been repeatedly mentioned in the Old Testament. Aden was then also known as a place of trade and commerce. (Ezekiel, xxvii. 23)

Of the towns in Yemen, Saba is frequently mentioned in the Holy Scripture. The Queen of Sheba presented herself to the court of Solomon (1 Kings, x. 1 & 13). Along with Saba other commercial towns of Yemen are also mentioned, such as "Roamah" (Ezekiel, xxvii. 29), Uzāl (which was then situated on the site now occupied by Sinai), "Havilah" (Genesis, xxv. 18) (which was a part of Ḥijāz in north Arabia and which was inhabited by Ishmaelites), and "Gur-baal" (2 Chronicles, xxvi. 7) (the location of which is not known). As the last town has been mentioned along with Palestine, it might have been situated somewhere in north Arabia.

The Hebrews were acquainted only with those tribes of Arabia with whom they were politically or commercially connected. The Midianites, the Ammonites, the Edomites, the Amalekites, and the Moabites were their neighbours and equals. Of the original tribes of Arabia, *i.e.*, the Qaḥṭānids and the Ishmaelites, peoples of Saba and Roamah belonging to the former tribe have been mentioned in the Old Testament. The Ishmaelites have been referred to in the Scripture as the people who had their trade in Arabia and Egypt (Genesis, xxxvii. 27) and who sometimes fought against the Hebrews jointly with the Midianites (Judges, viii. 24). Another name of the Ishmaelites was "Hajarites" and they have been referred to in the Old Testament by that name also (1 Chronicles, v. 10). Of the Ishmaelites, two clans, "the flocks of Kedar" and "the rams of Nebaioth", have also been mentioned in the Bible (Isaiah, lv. 7). Another Arabian tribe is referred to as "Ma'ūn", which the Arabs call "Ma'īn".

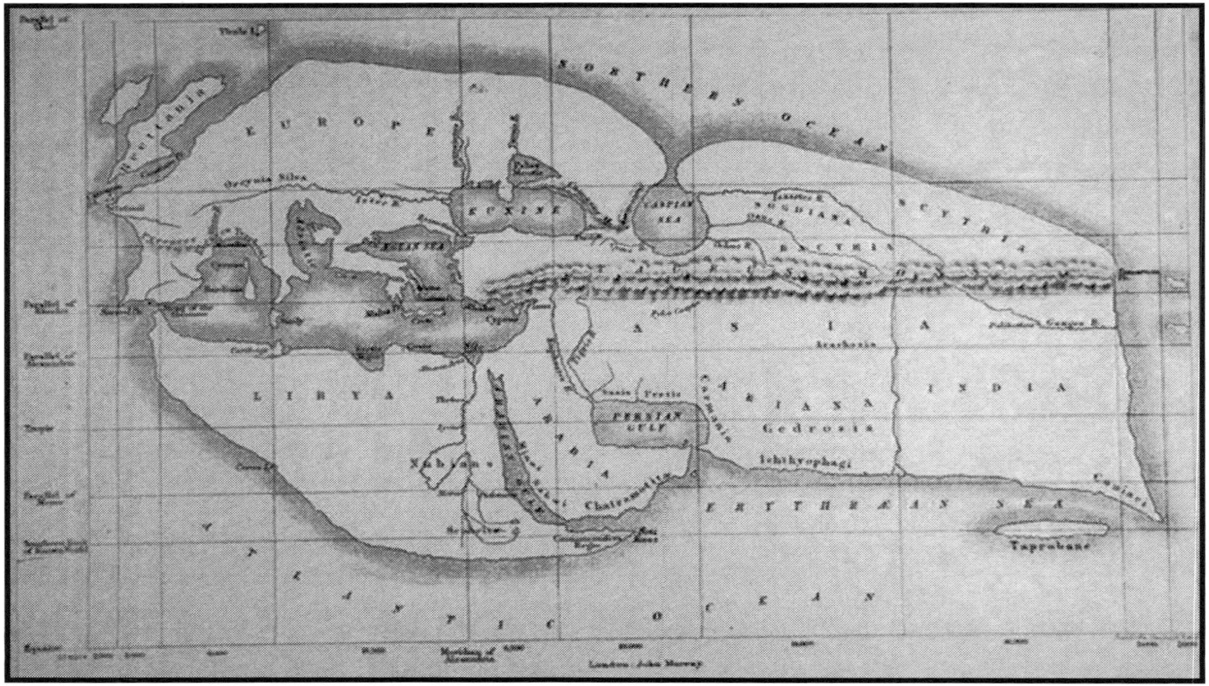

A reconstruction of a world map according to the Greek scholar Eratosthenes (276-194 BC) who introduced a technique to compute the first reliable determination of the size of the earth.

3

Arabia according to Classics (500–200 BC)

The first Greek who is accredited to have acquired some geographical knowledge was Homer who flourished in 1000 or 800 BC. He was a poet and made references to several towns and countries in his verses. He has referred to the Syrians under the name "Arimi" (connected with the Biblical Aram) and the Arabs under the name of "Erembi".[21]

The first Greek historian and geographer, Herodotus, (484-425 BC), knew something of Arabia and her people. But his knowledge was very limited, inasmuch as he thought that Arabia marked the end of human habitation on the south and that the river Nile was the western boundary of that country.[22] He did not know even this much that to the east of that country lies the Persian Gulf which divides Arabia from Persia.[23] He knew that there was a river on the west of Arabia but he named it as Arabian Gulf instead of the Red Sea.[24]

21. Bevan, *Ancient Geography*, p. 19.
22. H. Cary, *Herodotus*, Book III para. 107.
23. *Ibid.*, Book IV para. 39.
24. *Ibid.*, Book II para. 2.

Boundaries of Arabia

The Greeks' knowledge of the geographical condition of Arabia was substantially increased as a result of Alexander's conquests in the East in the third century BC. Now they ascertained that Arabia is bounded on the west by the Red Sea, on the east by the Persian Gulf, on the south by the Indian ocean, on north-east by the Euphrates and on north-west by Syria and borders of Egypt. They also included a large part of Sinai in Arabia. The Jews and Christians of the period also held the same view, as it appears from a letter of St. Paul (Galatians, iv. 25). But the geographers differ on the point, and this difference is mainly due to the absence of a natural boundary on the north-west of Arabia. Herodotus and Pliny extended its north-west boundary to the peninsula of Sinai and the Mediterranean Sea, while other geographers have confined it from the Dead Sea to Busra and Tadmur. The fact, however, is that owing to natural affinity and administrative similarity the above tracts have never been included in Arabia.

Divisions of Arabia

The early classical writers, such as Eratosthenes, Strabo and Pliny divided Arabia into two natural parts—southern and northern. But the most appropriate division of Arabia was given by Ptolemy in the second century CE which European geographers have followed up till now. He divided Arabia into (a) Arabia Petra, (b) Arabia Deserta and, (c) Arabia Felix. Arabia Petra included the north-west portion. In other words, it extended, on the west, from the border of Egypt to Busra, via the peninsula of Sinai and touched, on the north-west, Tadmur, Yahūdiyah, and Palestine. Arabia Deserta included the whole of the dimly-known interior, *i.e.*, its north-east boundary commenced from the Euphrates and Mesopotamia and terminated in the north-west frontier of Arabia Petra. Arabia Felix included the rest of the peninsula of Arabia which was bounded on the west by the Red Sea; on the east, by the Persian Gulf; on the south, by the Indian Ocean; and on the north, by Arabia Petra and Arabia Deserta. It included Ḥijāz, Yemen, Ḥaḍramawt, Oman, Bahrain Yamāmah and Nejd.[25]

The Greeks and Romans had conquered Arabia Petra and Arabia Deserta, and therefore they were fully acquainted with those parts. As they could not conquer Arabia Felix (which ever remained independent of foreign control), their knowledge of that part was extremely scanty. According to the researches of Dr Sprenger, Ptolemy has described in his *Geography* fifty four tribes, one hundred sixty-four towns, fifty mountains and four rivers of Arabia Felix. Stephenus and Pliny have also enumerated some towns and tribes of Arabia in their books, but most of these are now untraceable. (*see appendix I*)

The classical writers have described in detail Arabia Petra and Arabia Deserta because they were acquainted with them. But the difficulty is that the conquerors after having demolished old Arab towns founded new cities instead and gave them Greek names, as the following list will show:

1. Tadmur

It was a town near Palestine, which marked the northern boundary of Arabia. According to the Old Testament, this town was originally built by Solomon (1 Kings, ix. 18). The Romans captured it in 20 CE and changed its name to Palmyra.[26]

---

25. Forster, *Historical Geography of Arabia*, Vol. II. pp.
26. Josephus, (1822 edn.), Vol. I, p. 428.

2. Ribāt al-Mu'ab

This town was situated in Arabia Petra near the Dead Sea, and was the headquarters of the Moabite Arabs. The Romans changed its name to Areopolis, which was destroyed by an earthquake in 315 CE.[27]

3. Busra

It was a town situated near Ribāt al-Mu'ab and was the headquarters of the Edomite Arabs. The Romans converted its name to Bostra.

4. Al-Raqīm

It was called "Shiloh" in Hebrew and "Petra" in Greek. It was the capital of north Arabia first under the Midianites and afterwards under the Nabataeans. During the Roman period also it was an important town.

5. Ribāt al-'Ammon

It was the capital of the Ammonite Arabs on the north-eastern side of Arabia Deserta. The Greeks named it Philadelphia,[28] as it was rebuilt in the third century BC by king Philadelpheus.

Tribes of Arabia

The classical writers were acquainted only with those tribes of Arabia with whom they came in contact either politically or commercially. Of the Greek and Roman geographers of Alexandria, Pliny, Strabo, Diodorus and Ptolemy have mentioned some fifty or sixty tribes of Arabia, but their names have so radically changed in Greece, Alexandria and Rome that they now defy identification.

---

27. Bevan, *op. cit.*, p. 202.
28 Josephus, p. 192.

The following few tribes, however can be identified after scrutiny:

1. The 'Ād Iram

It was the oldest and most reputed tribe of Arabia that lived near Ḥaḍramawt. A great deal of this tribe had already perished before the Greek invasion. Only a section of it, i.e., followers of Prophet Hūd (Heber) had survived. The Greek geographers have mentioned this tribe under the name of "Adramitae" (*Adram* stands for 'Ād Iram, and *tae* means tribe.) Some people take the word "Adramitae" for Ḥaḍramawt. But it is open to objections, as that tribe is spelt in Greek as "Chatramotitai".

2. The Thamūd

Those of the tribe of the Thamūd who survived the Divine punishment were still living, during the Greek period, in their old residence at Midian near Ḥijāz. The Greek and Roman geographers have spelt this word in two ways— Thamydeni and Thamyditae.

3. The Ḥaḍramawt

In ancient time this tribe was equal in importance to the Yemenites both commercially and politically. The Greeks have spelt it as "Chatramotitai".

4. The Nabataeans

Two or three centuries before Christ, the country extending from Nejd to the coast of the Red Sea, 'Aqabah and Syrian Desert, was in the hands of the descendants of Nibṭ, a son of Ishmael. The Romans and Greeks had diplomatic relations with the Nabataeans, who lived in Petra.

5. The Kedarids

The family of Kedar, a son of Ishmael (from whom the prophet of Islam was descended), had been rulers of Ḥijāz from 1000 BC. The Greeks have spelt Kedar in different ways, most appropriate of which is "Cedarni" spelt by Pliny.[29] The tribes of Yemen, *i.e.*, Minaei (Ma'īn in Arabic) and Sabaei (Saba in Arabic), have been described by the Greeks in detail. They have also mentioned Omanitai (the Ammonites) and Gerrhaei (people of Qaryah situated in Yamāmah) in their geographical books.[30] Sometime before the advent of Islam, the Manādhira ruled in Ḥīrah and the Ghassānids in Syria under the suzerainty of the Persian and Roman Empires respectively. The Greek writers have given a detailed account of these peoples also.

29. Bevan, *op. cit.*, p. 178.

30. Forster. *op. cit.*, Vol. I, p. 244.

4

Arabia during the Qur'anic Period

The land

Though a peninsula, Arabia is generally described by its inhabitants as an island (Jazīrat-ul-'Arab). The Arabs have always regarded their country a central place of human habitation. D.G. Hogarth, Sir William Muir, and other modern scholars have also characterised Arabia as the heart of the Old World. The countries adjacent to Arabia are Persia on the east, India on the south, Abyssinia, the Sudān, and Egypt on the west, and Syria, Algeria, and Iraq on the north.

Boundary

According to Arab geographers, Arabia is bounded on the west by a portion of the Syrian Desert (extending from Balqā' to 'Ila near 'Aqabah); on the south-west by the Red Sea, Midian and the tract from Jeddah up to coast of Yemen; on the east, by the Indian Ocean, Aden and from Ẓafār upto Muhra; on the east, by the gulf of Oman, Persian Gulf, Muhra, Oman and the land from Bahrain up to Basrah and Kūfa; and on the north by the Euphrates and Balqa. In other words, Arabia is bounded, on the east, by the Persian Gulf and the gulf of

Oman; on the south, by the Indian Ocean, on the west by the Red Sea; on the north-west by the gulf of 'Aqabah, Syria, Palestine; and on the north-east by the Euphrates.

By making a comparision between Arabia as mapped by Arab geographers and Arabia as described by the Hebrews, Greeks and Romans, we find that the former is smaller in area in as much as it excludes the whole peninsula of Sinai and a portion of Arabia and Syria. The reason is not far to seek. The Greeks had captured the aforesaid territories and the Arabs could not take them back until the advent of Islam, and so they treated them as excluded from Arabia. As a matter of fact, they always formed part of Arabia owing to the close affinity they bore to that country.

Area

Arab geographers generally describe the area of a land in accordance with the time required in travelling from one of its ends to the other. Abu al-Fidā' has described in his book *Taqwīm-al-Buldān* that the country of Arabia can be traversed in seven months and eleven days. Arabia has never been surveyed in the modern sense of the term. Nevertheless, it is sure that it is a vast country, larger than the Indian peninsula and four times as large as Germany and France. From north to south (*i.e.*, from Port Sa'īd to Aden) it is 1,500 miles long, and from west to east (*i.e.*, from Port Sa'īd to the Euphrates) it is 600 miles wide and the area is 1,200,000 sq. miles.

Physical features

The vast country of Arabia is largely unpopulated, sandy and mountainous. It is a desert without water. There is practically no river worth the name. People generally depend on the streams running from the mountains, tanks and wells in the open field. The climate is hot and dry. The vast desert extending from Syria to Arabia on the north is the largest desert of Arabia, which the Arabs call "the Syrian Desert" and the non-Arabs "the Arabian desert". The second largest desert is "al-Dahnā'" (*i.e.*, sandy desert), which is also named "al-Rub 'al-Khālī" (solitary quarter). This desert lies in 11/2°N. Lat, and 2°E. Long., and its area is 250,000 sq. miles. Right across the country runs the largest chain of mountains from the south (Yemen) to the north (Syria) known as "Jabal al-Sarāt", its highest peak being 8,000 feet.

As said before, Arabia has no rivers worth the name; but this lack is amply compensated for by the streams which continually run from the mountains and which keep the skirts of mountains and valleys fertile. These streams running side by side develop into an artificial river, which, in its turn, either loses itself in the sands of the desert or flows into the sea. The kings of Arabia, in ancient times, had built dykes to check the flow of streams because they assumed a threatening attitude in case of a flood. The towns and provinces of Arabia which are situated on the coasts are generally fertile, and particularly so is the province of Yemen situated on the coast of the Indian Ocean and the Red Sea. This portion is, therefore, known among the Greeks as "Arabia fertile". Oman, Ḥaḍramawt, Nejd and Ṭā'if are the most productive parts of Arabia.

Products

The products of Arabia mostly consist in dates, apples and other kinds of fruits. Lands of cultivation are also met with here and there. Among the ancient nations, Arabia had been noted for her mines of silver and gold and perfumeries. Notices of the gold mines and frankincense of Arabia are found both in the Bible and classics. Hamdānī has mentioned the mines of Arabia in *Ṣifātu-Jazīrat-il-'Arab* in detail, while Burton has written a book on the subject, entitled *The Gold Mines of Midian*. The coasts of Oman and Bahrain are, so to speak, mines of pearls, where every year thousands of divers are engaged in fishing pearls. But Arab merchants have a very small share in the fruits of their labours, the lion's share going to the pockets of English companies. In 1910, the pearls of Bahrain alone were estimated at 1,200,000 pounds.

Of the animals found in Arabia, the horse is unparalleled in beauty and speed, and the camel is the most useful and valuable. Deer, lions and other animals are also found here. Herodotus has also mentioned the flying and deadly snakes of Arabia which is testified to by Moses's speech (Deut. viii. 15). However, they do not exist now.

Provinces

Arab geographers have divided their country, excluding Mesopotamia and Arabian Syria, into five provinces, *i.e.*, Tiḥāmah, Ḥijāz, Nejd, Yemen and 'Arūḍ. Many modern geographers treat Tiḥāmah as a part of Ḥijāz. The largest range of mountains in Arabia Jabal al-Sarāt forms the line of demarcation. The range which begins from the extreme north (the land of Syria) and ends in the extreme boundary of Arabia (Yemen) splits Arabia into two parts—eastern and western. The western part, which is smaller than the eastern in area, stretches in length from the borders of Syria to those of Yemen, and in breadth from the skirt of the above mountain to the coast of the Red Sea. This part is better known as Ḥijāz. The low-lying lands on the south of Ḥijāz (on the side of Yemen) are known as Tiḥāmah and Ghor (which literally mean low-lying lands). The eastern part which is generally high in level, extending from the mountain "Sarāt" to Mesopotamia is known as Nejd (which signifies high land). The hilly tract lying between Tiḥāmah and Nejd is called Ḥijāz because it stands as a barrier between the two countries (and the word "Ḥijāz" or "Ḥājiz" literally means screen or barrier). Yamāmah, Oman, Bahrain, and other towns lying between Iraq on the southern borders of Nejd and the Persian Gulf are known as 'Arūḍ, because this whole tract makes a curve line and "'Arūḍ" means curve. The southern part stretching from the coasts of the Red Sea up to those of the gulf of Oman (excluding Ḥijāz and 'Arūḍ) is known as Yemen, as this is a fertile and blessed land (and *Yumn* means blessing).

Province of 'Arūḍ

It comprises three districts, *i.e.*, Yamāmah, Bahrain and Oman.

1. Yamāmah

It is bounded, on the east, by Oman and Bahrain; on the south, by Aḥqāf (sandy desert); on the west, by Ḥijāz and a portion of Yemen; and on the north, by Nejd. The northern portion of Yamāmah is very fertile.

In ancient times Yamāmah was the home of the tribes of Ṭasm and Jadīs.[31] The well-known towns of the district were Ḥijr (or Qaryah) and Ja'da. The ruins of the buildings and forts of the above tribes had been extant in Yamāmah until the advent of Islam. The town Ḥijr, known also as Qaryah, was the headquarters of the above tribes. Zarqā', the blue-eyed woman, who is said to have possessed such a piercing sight that she was able to descry an enemy at a distance of three days' journey (*i.e.*, thirty miles away) belonged to Yamāmah. A little before the advent of Islam Yamāmah

31. Abū al-Fidā', *Geography*, Vol. I, p. 99.

was the residence of the famous tribe of Banū Ḥanīfah, an offshoot of the tribe of Bakr bin Wā'il). A deputation of this tribe waited on the Prophet in 8 H. and embraced Islam. The imposter Musaylamah, who was killed in war during the reign of Abū Bakr, belonged to the same tribe.

2. *Bahrain*

Also known as al-Iḥsā, is a coastal town. It is bounded by Yamāmah on the west and by the Persian Gulf on the east with Iraq above and Oman below it. As said before, Bahrain is noted for pearls, where thousands of divers remain engaged in fishing pearls every year.

The old history of Bahrain is that the Jadīs (who had occupied Yamāmah after defeating Ṭasm) were expelled by king Ḥisān of Yamāmah and fled to Bahrain. Afterwards the tribe of 'Abd al-Qays (descended from 'Adnān) occupied it. Some branches of Rabī'ah also lived here. In the sixth century CE, Bahrain was under the suzerainty of the Persians, and Manādhira, the Persian viceroy of Iraq and neighbouring towns, ruled over it. The famous Arab poet Ṭarafah was killed in Bahrain under the instruction of the descendants of Manādhira. In 6 H the ruler of Bahrain, Mundhir, son of Sāwī, embraced Islam with all his Arab subjects, and a deputation of the tribe of 'Abd al-Qays of Bahrain waited on the Prophet. The most remarkable event which took place in Bahrain in the Muslim age is that the Qarāmaṭah (the Carmathians), who were half-Muslims and half-Magians, chose this place as the centre of their political activities.

3. *Oman*

It is bounded, on the east, by the gulf of Oman; on the south by Bahrain; on the west, by Aḥqāf (sandy desert); and on the north, by Yemen. The places on the coast are rich and fertile. The largest mountain here is Akhḍar which is 3,000 metres high. The mountains of Oman abound in mines, its rivers in jewels, and its valleys in corn, fruits and fragrant herbs. It is also noted for good horses, cows and goats. Arab historians ascribe the town of Oman to 'Umān bin Qaḥṭān, but according to the Old Testament it should be ascribed to 'Umān bin Lūṭ. An offshoot of the tribe Azd, also known as Asad, lived here before Islam.

Province of Nejd

Nejd, which is a fertile high land in the centre of Arabia, is 1,200 metres above sea level. It is surrounded on three sides by deserts, and consequently secured from foreign aggression. It is bounded, on the north, by the Syrian Desert; on the west, by the desert of Ḥijāz; on the east, by Aḥqāf (sandy desert); and on the south, by the province of Yamāmah.

Nejd was formerly the home of the famous tribe Bakr bin Wā'il under the leadership of Kulayb, whose assassination led to the furious war between the tribes of Bakr and Taghlib which continued unabated for forty years. The Arabian State of Kindah, which claimed equality with the kingdom of Ḥīrah was included in the province of Nejd. When Qabād, the father of Nausherwan, adopted the religion of Mazdak, the rulers of Kindah (with a view to obtaining the Persian Emperor's favour against the Manādhira) also embraced that religion which ultimately led to their downfall.

The descendants of 'Adnān had occupied Nejd for a very long time. In the later period, the famous branch Ṭayy of the Kahlānī tribe settled in its mountainous places. Here also lived the clan of Ghaṭafān for whose chastisement the Prophet of Islam led an expedition in 4 H. The tribes of Hawāzin and

Salīm occupied the western side of Nejd. A certain clan of the tribe of Ḥaṭim also lived here.

Province of Yemen

Yemen is the most fertile and civilised province of Arabia. Before as well as after Islam it was the centre of learning and culture. Its past is wrapped in darkness. Ruins of buildings and forts are met with here in plenty, which testify to its past glory. The neighbouring empires of Rome, Persia and Abyssinia led successive invasions into Yemen, occasionally with success. The Greek and Roman historians have left an informative account of Yemen, and archaeological experts have also made contributions thereto.

The administrative boundary of the province of Yemen always varied in different times under different governments. It is bounded, on the south, by the Arabian Sea; on the west, by the Red Sea; on the north, by Ḥijāz, Nejd and Yamāmah; and on the east, by Oman and Bahrain. So far as our information of its past history goes, it was divided into a number of States; and several tribes, such as the Amalekites, the Minaeans, the 'Ādites, the Sabaeans and the Ḥimyarites founded their kingdoms here from time to time. They erected magnificent buildings here, the relics of which are still visible. Embankments were constructed here to control the springs of water from the mountains and utilise them for irrigation purposes. The most famous of these, Ma'rib, is mentioned in the Qur'an (34:15-16). India, Persia, Abyssinia, Egypt and Mesopotamia had their commercial relations with Arabia through the inhabitants of Yemen. It was the centre of trade in minerals and spices, and exported perfumeries to the civilised countries of the world.

The Abyssinians, nearly a century before Islam, captured Yemen and ruled over it for seventy years. They were at last displaced by the Persians. Bādhān, the Persian Governor of Yemen, embraced Islam in 7 H. and its inhabitants who had been mostly Jews accepted Islam through 'Alī bin Abī Ṭālib in 10 H. The famous tribe of Yemen, Hamdān, also accepted the new faith.

A large number of the old towns of Yemen are either barren or are sunk in sand. Some are populated, but their names have changed. The vastness of its area and the density of its population can be judged from the fact that it was, according to the historian Ya'qūbī, divided formerly into eighty-four districts. The well-known districts are the following:

1. *Ḥaḍramawt*

It lies on the coast of the Indian Ocean. It is bounded, on the north, by the Indian Ocean; on the south, by al-Rub 'al-Khālī (Solitary Quarter), and Aḥqāf; and on the west by Ṣan'ā. It was originally the home of Qaḥṭān (Yoqtan or Joktan), father of the Yemenite Arabs. The Old Testament has named one of his twelve sons as "Hazarmaveth" (Genesis x, 26) and so it is believed that this tract of land was named after its first inhabitant as Ḥaḍramawt. Here an independent State was set up by its people, a short account of which has been given by Ibn Khaldūn.[32] It was also the original home of the 'Ād and Thamūd but subsequently the former shifted to Aḥqāf and settled there.

2. *The Towns of Aḥqāf*

The "Rub 'al-Khālī" (Solitary Quarter) which extends over Yamāmah, Oman, Bahrain, Ḥaḍramawt and the western portion of Yemen is not worthy of human habitation. Some

32. *History*, Vol. II, p. 30.

people, however, settled in its vicinity, particularly in that part which stretches from Ḥaḍramawt to Najrān. Though this is a deserted land now, in old times it was the home of the famous tribe of 'Ād who met the Divine wrath and perished.

3. Ṣan'ā

This is the heart of the province of Yemen and centre of ancient Arabian civilisation. It is situated on the coast of the Indian Ocean and Red Sea, on the north-west corner of Arabia. Here the Minaeans, the Ḥimyarites and the Sabaeans established their large kingdoms, and it was here that the well-known dyke was built. Ẓafār, Uzāl, and Ma'rib were the headquarters of different governments. The Queen of Sheba also belonged to this place. The well-known castles such as Ghamdān, Nā'iṭ, Rubdah, Ṣarwāḥ and Madar had also been erected in Ṣan'ā, the ruins of which were witnessed by Hamdānī himself in the fourth century of the Islamic era.

4. Najrān

It is a small town between Aḥqāf and 'Asīr. In old times Bajīlah bin Nazār, descended from the Ishmaelites, settled here. Before the advent of Islam, Christianity was spread here by the Romans and Abyssinians. The Jewish kingdom of Yemen tried to convert the Christians to Judaism by force, but the Christian empires of Rome and Abyssinia always came to their rescue. In Najrān there was a magnificent church known among the Arabs as "Ka'bah Najrān". In 9 H a Christian delegation of Najrān waited on the Prophet of Islam, and was allowed to put up in the Prophet's mosque.

Province of Ḥijāz

Ḥijāz, which is situated on the coast of the Red Sea, is referred to in the Old Testament as Fārān, a place of divine manifestation. It is bounded, on the east, by Nejd; on the south, by 'Asīr; on the west, by the Red Sea; and on the north by Arabian Syria (or Arabia Petra). Right across the country runs a chain of mountains, known as Jabal al-Sarāt, from the south to the north, its highest peak being 8,000 feet. Streams running through the mountains keep the country fertile, which abounds in gardens and cultivable lands. That part is most fertile which is situated on the coast of the Red Sea and the rest is a sandy desert where agriculture is impossible. The largest coastal town of Ḥijāz is Jeddah, the port of Makkah, and the second largest coastal town is Yambu', the port of Madīnah. The important towns of Ḥijāz are Makkah, Madīnah and Ṭā'if.

1. Makkah

Makkah or Bakkah, also known as Umm al-Qurā, or the mother of towns, is the headquarters of the province of Ḥijāz. It was founded by Prophet Abraham where his son Ishmael migrated and where the Prophet of Islam was born. It lies in 21°38'N. Lat. and 40°9'E. Long.

It is nearly 330 metres above sea level. It is bounded on all sides by mountains. At present, it is nearly 30 kilometres long from east to west and nearly 1.5 kilometres broad from south to north.

In 2500 BC Makkah was a station of the commercial caravans. Approximately in 2000 BC Abraham and his son Ishmael together built here an altar in the name of God, which was named Ka'bah. The descendants of Ishmael had been supreme here until the rise of the Qaḥṭānids into prominence. In the later period Quṣayy, descended from Ishmael, succeeded in carving out a kingdom. He was the father and founder of the Qurayshites, who in the course of time became the masters of the town. They set up a government of their own, and various departments of the administration were entrusted to various heads of the family. Some of the Ishmaelite Arabs settled in the neighbouring towns of Makkah also.

2. *Madīnah*

It was originally called Yathrib. When it was adopted by the Prophet as his residence it became known as Madīnah al-Nabī or the City of the Prophet, which in the course of time became al-Madīnah or simply Madīnah. The town is 619 metres above sea level, and lies in 24°15'N. Lat, and 39°55'E. Long. It is situated on the north of the Equator. In summer its temperature rises up to 28°, and in winter it is 10° at day and -5° at night, and consequently in winter, water becomes frozen.

The town of Yathrib was first occupied by the Amalekites. They were followed by the Jews and then by two clans of the tribe of Azd known as Aws and Khazraj. The latter two were given the title of Anṣār (helpers) by the Prophet of Islam, as they welcomed the religion of Islam and extended their hospitality and support to the Muslim migrants.

3. *Ṭā'if*

Ṭā'if is, so to speak, a paradise of Ḥijāz. It is a fertile and healthy place where rich people of Ḥijāz generally pass their summer. Before the migration, the Prophet went to Ṭā'if to preach his religion but he was refused even a hearing. In 8 H it was laid siege to by the Prophet. In 9 H the head of the tribe embraced Islam which resulted in his assassination by his own people. But his voice did not prove a cry in the wilderness. The same year a delegation of that tribe waited on the Prophet and embraced Islam.

Other towns of Ḥijāz

The following places and towns of Ḥijāz are noteworthy:

1. *Jauf or Wādī al-Qurā*

On the north of Madīnah. It was inhabited by the Thamūd with Ḥijr as their capital. The Qur'an also mentions the town and its people. It is better known as Madā'in Ṣāliḥ (the towns of Ṣāliḥ) after its Prophet.

2. *Tabūk*

It was in this place that the Prophet of Islam stayed for some time to make preparations to meet the Roman attack, and in this connection he had to pass through the town of Ḥijr.

3. *Khaybar*

On the west of Madīnah. It was a stronghold of the Jews and centre of their political activities. In 7 H the Prophet of Islam conquered it.

4. *Madyan*

On the coast of the Red Sea opposite to Ḥijr. It was the home of Prophet Joshua, father-in-law of Moses, and the capital of the Madyan government.

At the commencement of Islam, the above towns were in the hands of the Jews, who had strong forts. They were, however, conquered by the Muslims during the Prophet's lifetime.

Arabian Syria

Arabian Syria, called by the Greeks Arabia Petra, comprises the whole tract running across Syria, Egypt, Syrian Desert, Ḥijāz and Nejd. This portion of Arabia has a historical importance.

It was here that Moses had the honour to converse with God, on the mount Sinai, and in its vicinity lies the promised land which was bestowed by God on the descendants of Israel (Banī Isrā'īl). The modern archaeological researches have considerably added to the importance of this territory. The Amalekites lived here and founded a very powerful kingdom which sometime extended its sway even over Ḥijāz, and which comprised Balqā', Oman, Busra and Tadmur, etc. The last mentioned town was noted for its commerce. The name of Zabā (Zenobia), a queen of this place, has been proverbially known among the Arabs. Sometime before the inauguration of Islam, the Ghassānids ruled over it with Busra as its capital. Hamdānī writes that after Islam the Banū 'Ajal settled in Arabian Syria extending up to Aleppo. The clan of Rabī'ah, a branch of the Ṭayy, also settled here, and several offshoots of the Jadhīmah flourished near Ghazzah. At the advent of Islam all these towns and villages were in the hands of the Arab Christians and Jews under the suzerainty of the Roman Empire.

Arabian Iraq

Arabian Iraq, known among the Greeks as Arabia Deserta, comprises the whole tract stretching across the Persian Gulf, the Euphrates, the Syrian Desert and Nejd. In oldern times, the Amalekites founded here a large kingdom. A clan of the Rabī'ah also lived here for some time. In the Muslim period, during the reign of the second Caliph 'Umar, the towns of Kūfa and Basrah were built here, which had long remained the centres of Arabic literature, civilization and culture.

Ibn Khaldūn writes that before Islam, the 'Abīd founded a state at Sanjār in Iraq near the Euphrates, whose last ruler was named Ḍizan bin Mu'āwiyah. The ruins of the buildings of this family are still extant in the plain of Sanjār. One of the branches of the Ṭāj, "Zubayd", flourished here, and a branch of the Banū 'Ajal spread all over Yemen and Iraq. At the advent of Islam the Arab family of Manādhira ruled over Iraq, under Persian suzerainty, with Ḥīrah, near Kūfa, as its capital.

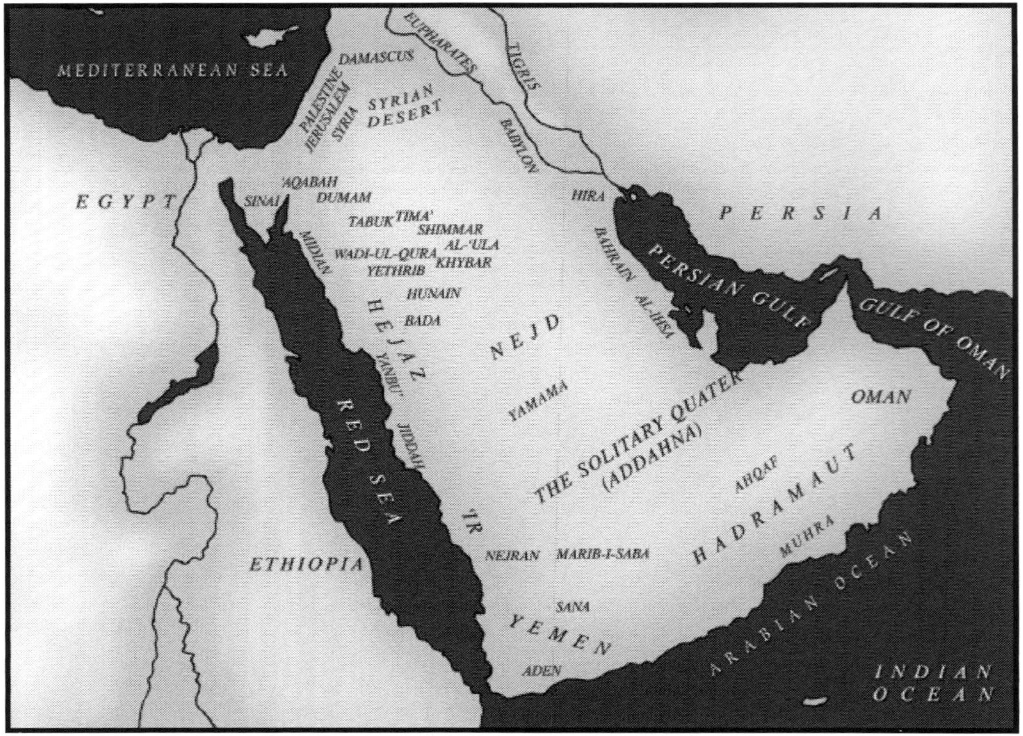

The land of the Qur'an

5
Arabia and Colonialism

Modern geographers divide Arabia broadly into two parts—Interior Arabia and Coastal Arabia. The former includes Bādiyah al-'Arab (Arabia Deserta), Nejd and al-Dahnā' (or the Solitary Quarter); and the latter comprises Syria, Palestine, Sinai, Ḥijāz, 'Asīr, Yemen, Ḥaḍramawt, Oman, al-Iḥsā' and Arabian Iraq.

Interior Arabia

1. Bādiyah al-'Arab

It covers that part of Arabia which lies to the north of Nejd and stretches between Iraq and Syria. The portion in the vicinity of Iraq is called the Desert of Iraq and that in the neighbourhood of Syria is named the Desert of Syria.

2. Nejd

It is bounded, on the north, by the deserts of Syria and Iraq; on the west, by Ḥijāz; on the east, by al-Dahnā' and al-Iḥsā'; and on the south, by 'Asīr and a portion of al-Dahnā'. Its area is 500,000 sq. miles, and its population is nearly two million.

3. Al-Dahnā'

This is a large desert extending from the south of Nejd to Oman, Ḥaḍramawt and Yemen. It is divided into three parts (a) Ṣayhid, which lies between the east of Yemen and north-west of Ḥaḍramawt, (b) Aḥqāf, which stretches on the north-east of Ḥaḍramawt, and (c) Wabār, which lies on the north of Muhra.

Coastal Arabia

1. Syria.

It is bounded, on the north, by the gulf of Alexandria and the Euphrates; on the east, by the Euphrates and the Desert of Iraq; on the south, by Ḥijāz and Palestine; and on the west, by the Mediterranean sea. Its area is 100,038 sq. miles, and its population is estimated at 2,750,000[33] people. Most of its inhabitants are Arabs. Among other nationalities, Turks and Kurds are prominent. The country is predominantly Muslim with a sprinkling of Jews and Christians. The chief towns are Aleppo (well-known as Halab), Antokio, Hims, Ba'labak and Damascus. The last-named is the capital of Syria.

2. Palestine

Formerly a part of Syria, it is now a separate state, with Jerusalem (Bayt al-Muqaddis) as its capital. Boundaries are: N., Phoenicia; E., the Dead Sea, S., the desert of Tīh; W., the Mediterranean sea. Its area is 9,270 sq. miles and contains nearly 800,000 people, of whom 600,000 are Muslims and the rest are Jews and Christians. The inhabitants are Arabs, but recently Jews of other nationalities have poured in Palestine in considerable numbers.

33. Based on data prevalent at the time of publication, *circa* 1930s.

3. *Sinai.*

Boundaries: N., Palestine and the Mediterranean sea; E., the gulf of 'Aqabah and borders of Ḥijāz and Syria; S., Red Sea, W., Suez Canal. Its area is 25,000 sq. miles and contains half a million people, most of whom are Arab Muslims.

4. *Ḥijāz*

Boundaries: N., Syrian Desert; E. Nejd; S., Mountains of 'Asīr; W., Red Sea. Its area is 96,562 sq. miles, and its population is something between 1/12 and 2 million. The inhabitants are Arab Muslims with a sprinkling of the permanently domiciled non-Arab Muslims. The chief towns of Ḥijāz are Makkah, Madīnah, Ṭā'if and Ma'ān.

5. *'Asīr*

Boundaries: N., Ḥijāz and Nejd; E., Mountains of Yemen; S., Yemen; W., Red Sea. It has an area of about 25,000 sq. miles and a population of over a million. The inhabitants are Sunnī Muslims. There are also some Shī'is.

6. *Yemen*

Boundaries: N., 'Asīr, Ḥijāz and Nejd; E., al-Dahnā' and Ḥaḍramawt; S., the Indian Ocean; W., the Red Sea. Its area is 73,813 sq. miles with a population of over four million. The people of Yemen are mostly the Shī'i Muslims of the Zaydī school (named after Zayd bin 'Ali). Some Jews are also met with here. The few Sunnīs are followers of Imām Shāfi'.

7. *Ḥaḍramawt*

Formerly a part of Yemen, it now forms a separate dominion. Boundaries: N., Oman and al-Dahnā'; E., the Indian Ocean; S., the Indian Ocean; W., Yemen. Its area is about 25,000 sq miles and contains nearly 600,000 people, all of whom are Sunnī Muslims of the Shāfi'ī school. The chief towns are Ẓafār, Mirmāt and Mukalla.

8. Oman

Boundaries: N., Bahrain; E., Gulf of Oman; S., Ḥaḍramawt; W., al-Dahnā'. It has an area of 80,000 sq. miles and a population of 160,000 people. All the inhabitants are the Khārijite Muslims.

9. Al-Iḥsā

Boundaries: N., Iraq; E., the Persian Gulf; S., Oman and al-Dahnā'; W., Nejd and Yemen. Its area is approximately 112,500 sq. miles, and its inhabitants number 350,000. It is also known as Bahrain and Hijr. The chief towns are al-Kuwayt and al-Hufuf.

10. Arabian Iraq

Iraq is divided into two parts—Northern and Southern. The former, where the Assyrians lived in by-gone days, is called al-Jazīrah (Mesopotamia); and the latter, which was peopled by the Babylonians in early times, is named Iraq al-'Arab (Arabian Iraq). Boundaries: N., al-Jazīrah and Kurdistān; E., Persia; S.E., Persian Gulf, S.W., Desert of Iraq and Nejd; W., the Euphrates and Syria. Its area is 115,875 sq. miles and has 2,900,000 people, of whom 1,500,000 are Shi'īs, 1,200,000 Sunnīs, and the rest are Jews and Christians. The people of Iraq are mostly Arabs by nationality, but a few Turks, Persians, Assyrians and Indians are found permanently domiciled here.

Politically, Arabia (or Jazīrah al-'Arab) at present is divided into several independent and semi-independent states under native and foreign rulers as shown below:

Turkish rule

The northern part of Syria (above Aleppo, *i.e.*, Halab) is under the Turkish Republic.

French rule

1. Syria proper (Northern and Eastern) with Damascus as its capital. This state was set up after the Great War under the French Mandate.
2. Syria (the Western part situated on the coast of the Mediterranean sea) with Ladhiqiyah and Tartus as its famous ports. This state was also formed after the Great War and is under the French influence.
3. Syria (South-western part in the vicinity of the mountain of Lubnān) with Ba'labak and 'Aliyah as its famous towns and Beirut as its chief port. This principality was established under the French suzarainty after the Great War.
4. Syria (South-eastern part in the neighbourhood of the mountain of Huran). It was placed under the French Protectorate after the Great War.

British rule

1. Palestine with Jerusalem (Bayt al-Muqaddis) as its capital. It was made a separate state under the British Mandate after the War.
2. Sharq al-Ardan with Oman as its capital. This principality stretching between Syria, Palestine and Ḥijāz on the north of the river Ardan was also set up under the British Protectorate after the War.

3. Aden: it has been under the British government since 1839 AD.
4. Mukalla (part of Ḥaḍramawt): it is a native state under the British suzerainty.
5. Masqat: it is an old native state on the coast of the Indian ocean. Formerly it was a mighty kingdom, but now it is a small principality under the English influence. The ruler is a Khārijite Muslim and is designated as Imam.
6. Bahrain: it is also a native state under the British influence.
7. Lahaj: it is a small native state, on the north of Aden, under the British protection.
8. Congregation of Petty States: a number of small states (probably eleven) have sprung up in the neighbourhood of Aden, and are now, more or less, under the British protection and influence. Most of their rulers get fixed allowances, monthly or annual, from the British government.

Egyptian rule

The Sinai Peninsula with an area of 25,000 sq. miles and a population of 50,000 people is under the Egyptian government.

Kingdom of Nejd and Ḥijāz

This is at present the strongest native kingdom in Arabia. Ibn al-Sa'ūd, King of Nejd, captured Ḥijāz in 1925 after defeating Sharīf Ḥusayn of Makkah. He has adopted various measures to consolidate the kingdom and purge the people of their evils, and has introduced a number of religious, social, moral and educational reforms in the country.

Kingdom of ʿAsīr

It was set up as a separate state by Muḥammad bin ʿAlī (Idrīsite) in 1330 H (1912 AD), but since 1345 H it has been under the suzerainty of the Saudi government of Nejd and Ḥijāz.

Kingdom of Yemen

It has been in existence ever since 280 H. It has now lost much of its past glory and power. Its ruler is designated as Imam, and belongs to the Zaydī school of the Shiʿīs.

Kingdom of Kuwait

It is a native state under the ʿĀl al-Ṣabāḥ with an area of 4,000 sq. miles and a population of 120,000 people.

Kingdom of Iraq

This state was established after the Great War under the British Mandate, but now it is almost an independent kingdom. From the above list it is evident that the country of Arabia is hopelessly torn into pieces, and that its unity, integrity and solidarity have gone for ever. ❁

PART II

The Peoples of the Qur’an

6
Introduction

Historians have divided human race into three great classes: (1) Aryan or Indo-European, *eg.*, Indians, Persians, English, French, etc.; (2) Turanian, or Mongolian, *eg.*, Chinese, Japanese, Mongolians, etc.; (3) Semitic, *eg.*, Arabs, Aramaeans, Hebrews, Assyrians, Chaldeans, Phoenicians, etc.

Some scholars have divided mankind according to their colours as follows: (1) White race, which includes the Semites and Europeans; (2) Black race, or Red race, which includes the natives of Africa; (3) Yellow race, which includes the Chinese, Japanese and the Turanian peoples.

Another division of human race (after the Deluge of Noah) is given in the Old Testament.[34] Noah had three sons, Japheth, Ham and Shem, and the descendants of these three brothers led to the three divisions of human race, as detailed below:

Sons of Japheth

They were seven: Gomer, Magog, Madai, Javan, Tubal, Meshech and Tiras.

---

34. Genesis.

Sons of Ham

They were four: Cush (father of Abyssinians), Mizraim (father of Egyptians), Canaan (father of Phoenicians), and Phut.

a. Cush had five sons, *i.e.,* Seba, Havilah, Sabtah, Raamah and Sabtechah.

b. Mizraim had seven sons, *i.e.*, Ludim, Anamim, Lehabim, Naphtuhim, Pathrusim, Casluhim (out of whom came Philistim), and Caphtorim.

c. Canaan had eleven sons, *i.e.*, Sidon, Heth, Jebusite, Amorite, Girgasite, Hivite, Arkite, Sinite, Arvadite, Zemarite and Hamathite.

Sons of Shem

They were five: Elam, Asshur, Arphaxad, Lud and Aram. Aram's sons were: Uz, Hul, Gether and Mash. Arphaxad had only one son named Salah, and the latter's son Eber had two sons: (i) Joktan (Qaḥṭān), father of the Qaḥṭānid Arabs, and (ii) Peleg, ancestor of Abraham.

How far the Biblical division of human race conforms to modern researches is not easy to say. A group of European scholars characterises it as unworthy of serious consideration. The rationalistic section of the Europeans holds that the division of human race given in the Bible is not genealogical or physiological, but geographical and political.[35] Those European scholars who aim at reconciling reason and tradition maintain that the Biblical accounts and the results of modern researches do not differ but only in name, and assert that the names mentioned in the Old Testament correspond to the old historical names either of peoples or countries, with some

35. *Encyclopaedia Britannica*, Vol. XXIV, p. 618.

modifications necessitated by the lapse of time and linguistic differences.[36] If we minutely observe the genealogical table of the Old Testament, we arrive at the conclusion that it only refers to the peoples and places of Palestine and its neighbourhood, such as, Assyria, Syria, Babylon, Chaldea, Media, Egypt, Damascus, Africa, Sinai and Arabia.

The Semites

Whatever be the viewpoint of the division of human race—whether we divide it genealogically, according to the Old Testament, (*i.e.*, Japheth, Ham and Shem), or philologically (*i.e.*, Aryan, Turanian and Semitic), or we divide it according to colours (*i.e.*, White, Red and Yellow)—the peoples inhabiting Arabia, Syria and Iraq are grouped in the same stock of human race. We may call them Banū Sām (descendants of Shem) after the Old Testament, or Semites according to philologists, or white peoples. The only difference between Banū Sām and Semites is that the former will include only those peoples who are descended from Sām (Shem) according to the Old Testament, but the latter will include all those peoples who used to speak or now speak the Semitic languages. Thus the descendants of Elam who resided on the borders of the Persian Gulf, and those of Lud who lived in Ludia, will be excluded from the Semitic races, because they never spoke Semitic; whereas the Phoenicians, the Babylonians, the Abyssinians, and the Amorites will be counted among the Semites as they always spoke Semitic.[37]

---

36. Bevan, *Geography of Torat.*
37. *Encyclopaedia Britannica*, "Semitic languages".

The Moabite stone or Mesha Stele, bearing an inscription by the 9th century BC Moabite King Mesha, is considered to be among the most valuable of semitic inscriptions.

7

The Original Home of the Semites

Arab historians are unanimous that the original home of the Semites was in Arabia. But the European scholars are divided on the question. Their views are given below.

1. The original home of the Semites was in Africa where the descendants of Ham, brother of Shem, could be traced even in the historic period. The argument for this theory is that there is a very close affinity between the Semitic and Hamitic languages, and that the Semites and Hamites, specially those of South Arabia, are similar in physique.

   This argument, however, is very strange. If one of two brothers, who resemble each other, lives in Africa, does it necessarily follow that the other brother also must live in Africa? Why is it not supposed that the Hamites after having lived with the Semites for a considerable time separated from them, and as a consequence of their common origin and long coresidence, they still retain some points of resemblance with their brothers, the Semites? The physical resemblance between the

South-Arabians (the Yemenites) and the Abyssinians (descendants of Ham) is quite natural because the latter are the mixed descendants of the former. Abyssinia was not a separate and independent country, but only a colony of the Yemenite Arabs.[38] This is why we find that ancient historians did not recognise Yemen and Abyssinia as two separate countries, but two parts of the same country, *i.e.*, Ethiopia.

2. The original home of the Semites was in Armenia and Kurdistān. No argument save a reference in the Old Testament has been advanced in support of this theory, and even that reference has been misunderstood (as the reader will find it later on). The most learned Orientalist, Nöldeke, therefore, declares this theory to be untenable.[39]

3. The original home of the Semites was in the lower portion of the Euphrates. This is the view of the Italian Orientalist, Professor Guidi, whose argument can briefly be described as follows:

   Every language must in the beginning consist of such words only as are necessary to express elementary requirements, and such words must be found, as a hereditary measure, in the different offshoots of that language. Now, those words which are commonly found in all the Semitic languages must guide us to locate the original home of their authors (*i.e.*, the Semites), and being guided by this principle we

38. *Encyclopaedia Britannica*, Vol. II, p. 264.

39. *Ibid.*, Vol. XXIV, p. 620.

come to the conclusion that the original home of the Semites was in the lower portion of the Euphrates.

Nöldeke refutes this view by saying (a) that the common words for elementary necessaries have been wiped out of existence by the lapse of time, and (b) that the very assumption, that all the words for elementary necessaries must be common in the principal language and its offshoots, does not tally with reason, *eg.*, tent, boy, man, old, and some other words which are most elementary are not common in all the Semitic languages, and (c) that those words which are common between the Semites of the north and those of the south must, according to Professor Guidi's theory, have come into existence in their original home, but the fact is that such words can hardly be traced near the Euphrates.

Before Guidi the same sort of argument was advanced by Von Kremer, who held that the ancient home of the Semites was near the Oxus and Jaxartes in Central Asia. That two conflicting conclusions could be derived from the similar data is enough to refute both of them.

4. Arabia was the birthplace of Banū Sām (sons of Shem). This theory which is substantiated by facts and arguments finds favour with a large number of historians of Europe and America, such as De Goege, Schrader, Winckler, Tiele, Meyer, Sprenger, Nöldeke, Keane, Robertson Smith, Samuel Laing, W. Wright Sayce, W.R. Rogers and so on.

The argument in support of this theory can be put briefly as follows:

a. History proves that many early nations originally belonging to Arabia settled in other lands.

b. Of all the Semitic languages Arabic is the nearest to the original Semitic language.

c. The physical structure of the Arabs bears striking resemblance to the Semitic structure.

d. The nomadic mode of Arabian life is a relic of the primitive and antiquated life of the Semites.[40]

Let me quote the views of some well-known historians and philologists who hold that Arabia was the birthplace of the Semites:

1. The Semitic traditions conclusively prove that Arabia was the primitive home of the Semites. Arabia is the only tract of land which has ever since remained Semitic. Racial characteristics, religious fanaticism, aloofness from foreigners and nomadic mode of life, prove the birthplace of the Semites to have been in a land of desert—Sayce.[41]

2. According to my conviction all the Semites can be traced to Arabia. They divided themselves into a number of tribes and sections. Who knows how many tribes preceded the Canaanites we meet with in the beginning of history—Dr Sprenger.[42]

40. W.R. Rogers, *History of Babylon and Assuria*, Vol. I, pp. 306-307.

41. A.H. Sayce, *Assyrian Grammar.*

42. A. Sprenger, *Geography of Ancient Arabia*.

3. Religious anecdotes, philological researches, historical and geographical evidences prove conclusively that the original home of the Semitic races was in Arabia—Schrader.

4. The first home of the Semites was Central Arabia, whence different clans migrated to Syria, Babylon, Oman and Yemen, pushing off their predecessors towards Kurdistān, Armenia and Africa—De Goege.

5. It is almost clear that they (the Assyrians) came from Arabia, the birthplace of the Semites, though they afterwards changed their nomadic life (and adopted a purely agricultural mode of life) in accordance with the local environments and circumstances—Heeren.[43]

6. It will take us some time to decide which of the views held by different scholars is correct, but at present I agree with Schrader and De Goege (quoted above)—W. Wright.[44]

Professor W.R. Rogers says:

> Whence these invaders (the Semites) came is not certain. It has been thought by some that they came from the north-east through the passes of the Kurdistān mountains, and that Babylonia was the land in which they had their first national development and from which they spread over western Asia to make great careers as Arabians, Canaanites and Aramaeans. This view, once stated and supported with suppressing learning, is now almost abandoned, and but few

43. A.H.L. Heeren, *Historical Researches of Ancient Commerce and Politics*, Vol. I, p. 292.

44. W. Wright, *Grammar of Semitic Languages*.

> great names may be cited among its adherents. A second view finds the original home of the Semites in Africa either in the north-eastern or north-western part of the great continent. It will be idle to deny that strong linguistic support for this view may be found in the recognised affinity between the Semitic languages and Egyptian, Coptic, Berber and the Kushite (Bisharee, Galla, Somali, etc.) languages. But when all has been said in favour of this view, there still remain more potent considerations in favour of a third view, that the original home of the Semites was in Arabia, out of which they came in successive waves of migration to find larger and more bountiful lands in Babylonia, Mesopotamia, and even in the far western land of Canaan. This latter view seems ever to find fresh supports in the newer facts and to me it is clearly the best solution of the problems.[45]

Samuel Laing writes:

> Our point seems sufficiently clear; that wherever may have been the original seat of the Aryans, that of the Semites must be placed in Arabia. Everywhere else we can trace them as an immigrating or invading people, who found prior populations of different race, but in Arabia they seem to have been original. Thus in Chaldea and Assyria, the Semites are represented in the earliest history and traditions coming from South, partly by the Persian Gulf and partly across the Arabian and Syrian Deserts. In Arabia alone we find Semites and Semites only, from the very beginning.[46]

The most authentic writer on the subject, Nöldeke, writes in the *Encyclopaedia Britannica*, in his article on "Semitic languages":

---

45. Heeren, *op. cit.*, Vol. I, p. 452.
46. Samuel Laing, *Human Origin.*

> Some prominent scholars consider the birthplace of the Semitic race to have been in Arabia. There is much that appears to support this theory. History proves that from a very early period tribes from the deserts of Arabia settled on the cultivable lands which border them and adopted a purely agricultural mode of life. Various traces in the language seem to indicate that the Hebrews and the Aramaeans are originally nomads and Arabia with its northern prolongation (the Syrian Desert) is the true home of nomadic people. The Arabs are also supposed to display the Semitic character in its purest form, and their language is, on the whole, nearer the original Semitic than are the languages of the cognate races... We willingly admit that the theory which regards Arabia as the primitive seat of all Semites is by no means untenable.[47]

Another writer in his article on "Arabia" in the *Encyclopaedia Britannica* writes:

> Arabia is a land of Semites, and is supposed by some scholars to have been the original home of the Semitic peoples. Although this cannot be said to be proved, the studies, linguistic and archaeological, of Semitic scholars have shown it to be probable. The dispersion from Arabia is easy to imagine. The migration into Babylonia was simple, as there are no natural boundaries to separate it from north-east Arabia, and similar migrations have taken place in historic times. That of the Aramaeans at an early period is likewise free from any natural hindrance.[48]

So far we discussed the question of the original home of the Semites from the view points of language, customs, practices, physical resemblance and natural evidences. Now

---

47. *Encyclopaedia Britannica*, Vol. XXIV, p. 620.
48. *Ibid.*, Vol. II, p. 263.

let us approach the subject from the historical standpoint. The oldest history on the subject is the Old Testament and there we find: "And the whole earth was of one language, and of one speech. And it came to pass, as they journeyed from the east, that they found a plain in the land of Shinar [Babylonia]; and they dwelt there.... So the Lord scattered them abroad from thence upon the face of all the earth: and they left off to build the city. Therefore is the name of it called Babel" (Genesis, xi. 1-2, 8-9).

Now the question is: What is meant here by the "east"? Commentators of the Old Testament have not yet been able to give a definite answer to the question. It is, however, generally assumed that the east here means Armenia, because the mountain on which the Arc of Noah anchored is mentioned in the Old Testament under the name of Ararat which is supposed to be situated in Armenia. But the difficulty is that Armenia is not situated on the east, either of Babylon or of Palestine. To remove this difficulty some say that Moses lived in Egypt and Arabia, and Armenia lies on the east of these countries; while others say that as man first of all knew the eastern horizon only (the east being the rising place of the sun), Armenia has been referred to as an eastern country. It is hardly necessary to say that these suggestions are not worthy of serious consideration.

From the Biblical statement it is clear that Babylon was not the first residence of the Semites and that they migrated to that country from the east. In the language of the Bible the term "east" generally stands for the east of Palestine which was the place of the compilation of that Holy Book, *i.e.*, Babylon and Arabia. Babylon being the place to which they (the Semites) migrated from the east, the term "east" cannot but refer to the other country, *i.e.*, Arabia (the place from which they migrated).

Our most ancient source of information after the Old Testament is *The Antiquities of the Jews* by Josephus, which is, in some sense, a commentary of the Old Testament. There we find: "They (the semitic races) extended from the Euphrates up to the Indian ocean." The land between the Euphrates and the Indian Ocean cannot be any other country than Arabia.

Another point to be noticed is that the Arabs alone have claimed that their country was the first home of the Semites, and this claim which has been substantiated by arguments and evidences is not disputed by any other people. Naturally, therefore, the Arabs' claim must be accepted as true.

The historian Ibn Qutaybah (d. 276 H.) writes:

> Sām bin Nūḥ (Shem, a son of Noah) occupied the land lying between Makkah and the neighbouring territories, *i.e.*, Yemen, Ḥaḍramawt, Oman, Bahrain, Bubrain, Dabār, Daw and Dahnā'.[49]

The historian Ya'qūbī (d. 280 H.) writes:

> The descendants of Sām (Shem) had Ḥijāz, Yemen and other lands in their occupation.[50]

The Qur'an, therefore, rightly characterises Makkah as "Umm al-Qurā" (mother of towns), as it says:

> *So that you may warn "the mother of towns" (i.e., Makkah) and the people who live in its neighbourhood. (6:92)*

49. *Kitāb al-Ma'ārif* (Egypt), p. 10.
50. *Tārīkh* (Lyden), p. 17.

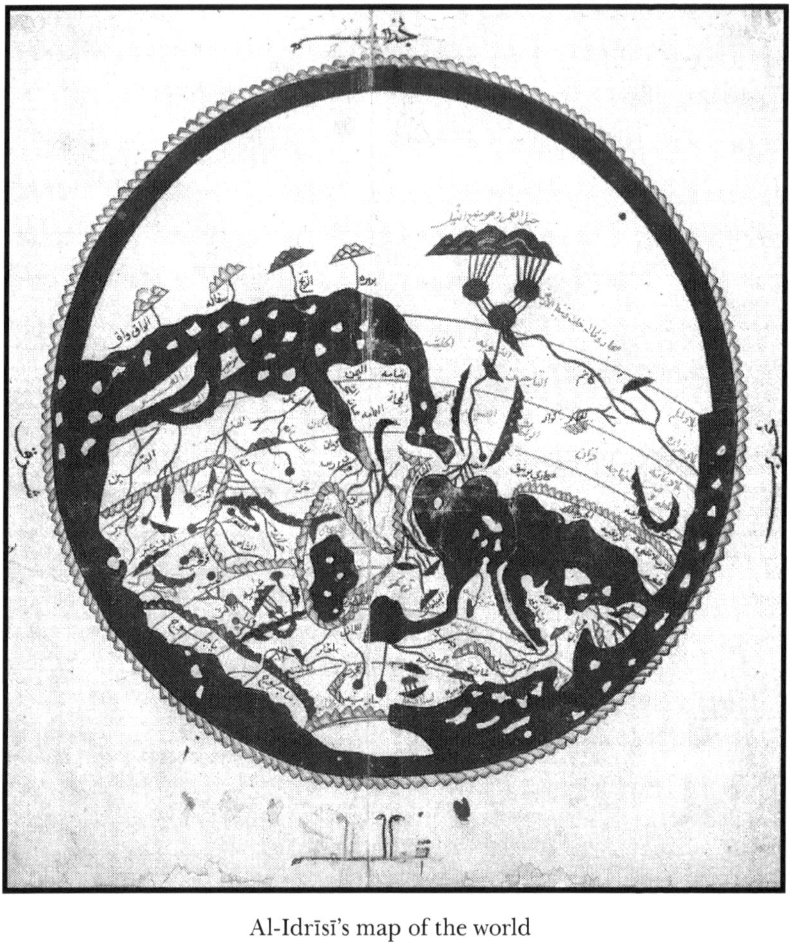

Al-Idrīsī's map of the world

8
The Migration of the Semites

There have been four great upheavals in the history of Arabia. Firstly, in about 3000 BC, a large number of tribes migrated from Arabia and spread to Babylon, Assyria, Egypt and Phoenicia. Secondly, in 1500 BC, the Edomites, the Moabites and the Midianites of Arabia left their home for the neighbouring territories. Thirdly, the Minaeans and the Sabaeans migrated to some foreign lands. Fourthly, in the seventh century CE (first century H.), the Arabs under the banner of Islam spread to foreign countries far and wide.

At present we are concerned only with the first upheaval of Arabia — the emigration of the Semitic peoples from their primitive home. The views and theories of several European and American scholars have already been given above, and more evidences in support of the theory of the Arabian origin of the Semites are given below.

In 3000 BC we find the Semitic peoples migrating from their original home. The Canaanites lived in Syria where the Phoenicians, after having left the coast of the Persian Gulf (Bahrain), established commercial towns, improved the navigation system, and put an end to the Aegean civilization.

They afterwards carved out a sea-route to Europe. Then the Hyksos invaders attacked Egypt where they succeeded in establishing a kingdom of their own. But the history of the Bedouins of Arabia Deserta is still obscure. In the course of time, they took to building towns and founding kingdoms, and their only source of income was commerce.[51]

The Semitic races of the north, *i.e.*, the Armenians, Assyrians and Canaanites, after having separated from the cognate races, came to Babylon and lived there for a long time as a united body. It appears that the Armenians first separated, then the Canaanites, and at last the Assyrians. Just in this period some of these tribes migrated to the south and settled on the coast of the Arabian peninsula, whence a section of them advanced to Africa and settled in Abyssinia.[52]

The above assertions are corroborated by Muslim historians. Ibn Qutaybah, after describing the separation of the different clans of the descendants of Sām (Shem), writes:

From among them (the Semites) were the Amalekites[53] (who were composed of different tribes) who spread in different countries and among them were the kings of Egypt and Babylon.[54] (*see appendix II*)

51. Huart, *Introduction to History of Arabia.*

52. Schrader (W. Right, *Grammar of Semitic Languages*, p. 9).

53. The following etymological explanation of the word Amalek is given in the Encyclopaedia of Islam, Vol. I, p. 377: "Hubert Grimme has given an explanation free from objection of this name Melukh from the Old Testament 'Amalek' (broken plural of a singular Amluk) with a prosthetic vowel hardened as often in Arabic to *'ayn* and with the rendering (for which analogies may also be found) of Kaf by an aspirate sounding like *ghain* in Sumerian: Thus there would really be epigraphic sources for the existence of this first of the nations (Num. xxiv. 20) as early as the second half of the third millennium BC".

54. *Kitāb al-Ma'ārif*, p. 10.

Ibn Khaldūn writes:

> The Semites had many kings and kingdoms in Arabia, and some of their tribes extended their sway up to Syria and Egypt.[55]

55. *Tārīkh*, Vol. II p. 259.

Greek historian Strabo (63–24 BC), whose work on geography touches on the Nabataeans and makes reference to Najrān and Ma'rib, the two well-known towns of Arabia.

9

The First Chain of the Semites

By the first chain of the Semitic peoples are meant the original inhabitants of Arabia, who for various reasons migrated to Babylon, Egypt and Syria. Arab historians call them as Umam Bā'idah (the destroyed races), as they perished after migration. Some refer to them as 'Arab 'Āribah (unmixed Arabs). The Jews and some other people have wrongly given them the name of the Amalekites.

The European archaeological experts have not been able to give separate names to the different chains of the Semitic races. They vaguely term them as Semites. The Arabs, however, name them separately.

The 'Ād, the Thamūd, the Jurhamites, the Lakhmids, the Ṭasm, and the Jadīs are the most ancient races of Arabia. The 'Ād who were greatest and most powerful people dominated over the whole of Arabia. According to the Arabian traditions, they had their kingdoms in Arabia, Babylon and Egypt. The Arab historians in general have traced the genealogy of the 'Ād and other cognate races to Aram, son of Shem. But the problem as to which clan descended from which branch of the Aramaic race is difficult to solve. The genealogical experts so much differ in their views that it is well nigh impossible to reach a definite conclusion. I quote below two genealogical tables as given by Ibn Qutaybah in *Kitāb al-Ma'ārif* (one of the earliest sources), (Egyptian ed., p. 10) and by Qalqashandī in his book Sabā' ik al-Dhahab (one of the latest sources). (Bombay edn., pp. 13, 14):

	Ibn Qutaybah	Qalqashandī
1.	'Amālīq, b. Lavādh, Aram, b. Sām	'Amlīq, b. Lavādh, b. Sām
2.	Jadīs, b. Lavādh, b. Aram, b. Sām	Jadīs, b. Aram, b. Sām
3.	'Ād bin Uz, b. Aram, b. Sām	'Ād, b. Uz, b. Aram, b. Sām
4.	Thamūd, b. Gether, b. Aram, b. Sām	Thamūd, b. Gether, b. Aram b. Sām
5.	Ṭasm	Ṭasm, b. Lavādh, b. Sām

The famous historian Ibn Khaldūn has tried to solve the difficulty but with little success. This much, however, is certain that the Semites were descended from Sam (Shem) and that the Aramaic element was predominant in them. The Arabic language contains many Aramaic words and phrases.[56] The word "Makkah" is also Aramaic.[57] The inscriptions of the Thamūd available so far are also in the Aramaic character.[58] The Thamūd were called Thamūd Iram[59] and the 'Ād as 'Ād Iram. In this connection Ibn Khaldūn writes: Formerly the 'Ād were known as 'Ād Iram. When they perished, the Thamūd

56. P. Arnold, *Sawā-'us-Sabīl.*
57. Jurji Zaidan, *al-'Arab Qabl al-Islām*, p. 240.
58. *Encyclopaedia Britannica*, Vol. XXIV, p. 626.
59. Ibn Khaldūn, *Tārīkh*, Vol. II, p. 71.

were called Thamūd Iram, and when the latter also perished, the Nimrūd were named as Nimrūd Iram.[60]

If we analyse the Semitic peoples, we find that the most powerful clan was the 'Ād. Some European authors of ancient history have characterised the 'Ād as fictitious and mythological, but they are entirely mistaken. The recent discoveries have conclusively proved that the original inhabitants of Arabia (*i.e.*, Semitic races) were numerically very strong and established great kingdoms in Babylon, Egypt, and Syria. The Arabs call them collectively as 'Umam Bā'idah, and separately as 'Ād, Thamūd, Ṭasm, Jadīs, *etc.* The most authentic source of our information is the Qur'an which says:

> *Did you not see what your God did to the 'Ād Iram?* (Qur'an, 89:6-7)[61]
>
> *Remember (O 'Ād!) that God made you successors of the people of Noah.* (Qur'an, 7:69)

The famous French historian Sedles writes: "The history of Umam Bā'idah (destroyed races) is unreliable. What is known or is presumed to be known is the fact that the 'Ād had Egypt and Babylon in their possession in 2000 BC and that they were known at that time as Hyksos (the shepherd-kings)."[62] It is needless to say that this presumption is amply justified by historical evidences and archaeological discoveries.

---

60. *Ibid.*, p. 7.
It is noteworthy here that all the places where the Semitic peoples settled were, in the course of time, named after Aram, and so the Old Testament refers to Mesopotamia (Iraq) as "Aram Nahrain" and "Padan-aram", Syria as "Aram" and "Aram-i Damuscus"; and north Arabia as "Aram-i-Arab". Moreover, all the old inscriptions that have been found in Babylon, Assyria, Syria, Canaan, Phoenicia and north Arabia are either Aramaic or full of Aramaic words.

61. The verse clearly shows that the 'Ād were descended from Aram (son of Shem, son of Noah).

62. *History of Arabia.*

Tema Stone: A 6th century BC stone with Aramaic inscriptions found in Tema, northwestern Arabia

10

The 'Ād

The term 'Ād

Among the Semitic languages Hebrew is the oldest. The Hebrew word for 'Ād means "high and famous" and the words *Aram* and *Shem* also bear the same meaning. In Arabic the word *Aram* literally means a hill and milestone. In the Old Testament the word *'Ād* is used for the males and *'Ādah* (Genesis, xxxvi. 2) for females, which fact shows that even in early times the term *'Ād* was frequently in use.

Period of the 'Ād

Date system was not in vogue during the pre-Islamic period of Arabia and, therefore, the time of Umam Bā'idah is difficult to ascertain. But in view of the fact that Arab historians have described 'Ād as the son of Uz, son of Aram, son of Shem, son of Noah, it is likely that the 'Ād lived before 3000 BC. The Qur'an has also referred to the 'Ād as successors of the people of Noah, as it says: "Remember (O 'Ād!) that God made you successors of the people of Noah" (Qur'an, 7:69). Again, "Verily, God destroyed the 'Ād, the first" (*i.e.*, the first chain of the Semites). From the latter verse not only can the time of the 'Ād be fixed but also our theory is confirmed that the first chain of the Semites and the 'Ād were one and the same people. It is, however, generally admitted that the real progress of the Semites began either in 2200 or 2000 BC, the period during which they invaded Egypt and Babylon. The period of the 'Ād Iram, therefore, may be said to have begun from 2200 BC. We also find that in 1500 BC another power came into being in Yemen (and that after the advent of Moses whose time preceded 1500 BC), and so the 'Ād had been completely wiped out of existence in that period. Consequently we can fix the time of the 'Ād as beginning from 2200 BC and ending before 1500 BC (we may roughly say, in 1700 BC). The Qur'an mentions the 'Ād to have perished before the time of Moses and Pharaoh, as it says:

> *O my people! surely I fear for you the like of what befell the Hordes, the like of what befell the people of Noah and 'Ād and Thamūd and those after them. (So said a follower of Moses to Pharaoh and his people.)* (Qur'an, 40:30-31)

Some of the believers among the 'Ād, however, continued to live until the beginning of the Christian era, and the Greeks have referred to them as "Oditai" ('Ād) or "Adramitai" ('Ād Iram) in their account of the inhabitants of Ḥaḍramawt and Yemen. For distinction the 'Ād of the first period are referred to as the 'Ād I and those of the second period as the 'Ād II.

The Home of the 'Ād

The 'Ād lived in the best part of Arabia *i.e.,* Yemen and Ḥaḍramawt, spreading from the coasts of the Persian Gulf to the borders of Mesopotamia.[63] Yemen was their capital,

63. Ibn Qutaybah, *Ma'ārif* (Egypt), p. 10.

which extended up to Iraq on the coast of the Persian Gulf, and from which place they used to travel far and wide with ease and peace.[64]

Kingdoms of the 'Ād

Arabia has practically no rivers and, therefore, her people frequently migrated to the neighbouring countries. As the Arabian peninsula is surrounded by water on the south, on the west, and somewhat on the east also, the Arabs usually frequented the countries on the north and east, such as Babylon, Syria, and Persia.

64. According to S. Laing (*Human Origin*, pp. 33, 39) the favourite route of the 'Ad was from Arabia to Iraq and thence to different countries.

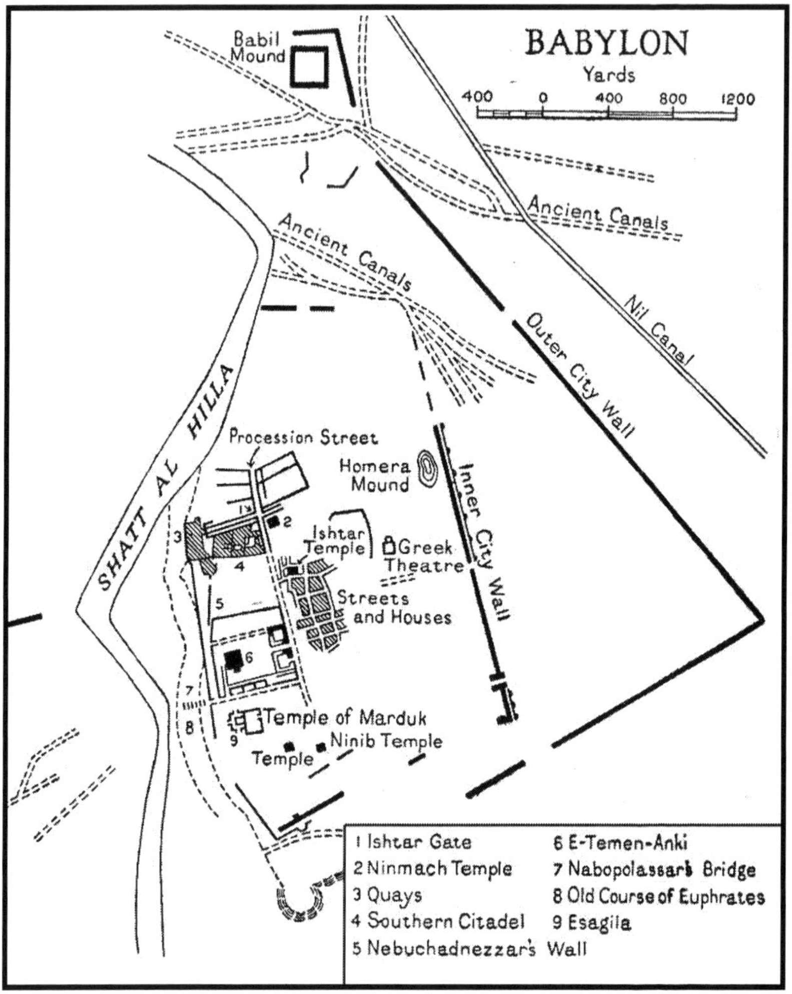

Ground plans of Babylon

11
Arabs outside Arabia (4000–1900 BC)

We can study the Arabs (or 'Ād I) outside Arabia under the following heads: (1) the 'Ād in Babylon; (2) the 'Ād in Egypt; (3) the 'Ād in other countries; (4) the 'Ād as described in the Qur'an.

The 'Ād in Babylon

That the Arabs once ruled over Babylon is admitted by the Babylonians themselves and is confirmed by modern researches. Different evidences in support of this view are given below.

The Arabs' evidence

Ibn Qutaybah writes in *Kitāb al-Ma'ārif*:[65]

> From among them [the Arabs] were the Amalekites (who were composed of different tribes) who spread in different countries, and among them were kings of Egypt and Babylon.

Ibn Khaldūn says:

> The 'Ād and the Amalekites ruled over Iraq. It is said that when the descendants of Ham opposed them, they migrated from Babylon to Arabian peninsula.[66]

65. p.10.
66. *Kitāb al-'Ibar* (*Egypt*), Vol. II, p. 18.

Ibn al-Nadīm writes:

> They left Iraq for Ḥijāz (at the time of their migration from Babylon) in fear of the Hamitic kings.[67]

The Persians' evidence

The Persians assert that the Arabs were the ancient rulers of Iraq and Babylon, and that after Jamshīd (who was a contemporary of Shem, son of Noah) Ḍaḥḥāk, an Arab, occupied those countries. The Arabs also testify to it, as the celebrated historian al-Ṭabarī states:

> The people of Yemen claim that king Ḍaḥḥāk bin 'Alwān belonged to their nationally.... It is also narrated that Ḍaḥḥāk was identical with Nimrūd during whose reign Abraham was born, and that it was he who ordered him to be burnt.[68]

Firdawsī, a most authentic narrator of the Persian annals, has described the 1000 years' long administration of Ḍaḥḥāk in his *Shāhnāmah*.

The Old Testament's evidence

The predecessors of the Israelites lived in Babylon before the time of Abraham, and from 2500 BC they had been in close relation with the inhabitants of that country. In the Old Testament we find:

> And the sons of Cush; Seba, and Havilah, and Sabtah, and Raamah, and Sabtechah: and the sons of Raamah; Sheba and Dedan. And Cush begat Nimrod; he began to be a mighty one in the earth. He was a mighty hunter before the world: wherefore it is said, even as Nimrod the mighty hunter before the Lord. And the beginning of his kingdom was Babel, and

67. *Al-Fihrist* (Europe), p. 28.

68. *Tārīkh*, pp. 202, 205.

Erech [Iraq] and Accad, and Calneh, in the land of Shinar. (Genesis, x. 7-10)

The learned German historian Duncker in explanation of the above Biblical statement says that the term *Cush* used in the Genesis includes all those nations who lived in the southern territories, *eg.*, Ethiopians and Nubians; and by the tribes of the southern Arabia are meant those descendants of Cush who founded Babylon and also settled on the coast of the Persian Gulf.[69]

The Babylonians' evidence

A Chaldean historian of Babylon named Brushes, who flourished in 400 BC, wrote a history of ancient Babylon. The book is lost, but quotations from it are frequently given by the Jewish and Greek authors. Of many quotations one relates to kings of Babylon, according to which the number of Arab kings (of Babylon) was nine and the duration of their reign was 225 years. The following is the table of the ancient kings of Babylon:

No. of Kings	**Dynasties**	**Duration of reign (*years*)**
10	Kings before the Deluge ...	432,000
86	Kings after the Deluge ...	34,000
8	The Usurpers of Media ...	224
11	Unknown kings ...	248
49	Chaldean kings ...	458
9	Arab kings ...	225

69. *History of Antiquity*, Vol. I, p. 249.

Archaeological evidence

All that we could gather from the statements of the Arabs and Babylonians is that in some remote antiquity a section of the Semites ruled over Iraq. But now with the help of archaeology the lost civilisation of Babylon is coming to light and every stone that has been discovered in Babylon and Assyria bears an eloquent testimony to their past glory.

The inscriptions that have been discovered in Babylon can be linguistically divided into: (a) Semitic and (b) non-Semitic. They help us to trace the nationality of the early inhabitants of Babylon. Some of these inscriptions contain the dates of the kings and others do not, and in the latter case dates have been suggested by analogy and external evidences. Non-Semitic inscriptions appear to be of earlier dates than the Semitic ones, which shows that the non-Semitic races preceded the Semites in Babylon. The language of the non-Semitic inscriptions was Sumerian or Akkadian, and hence we may infer that they relate to the Sumerians or Akkadians who were, in all probability, Tūrānian in origin. The language of the non-Semitic inscriptions is called "Akkadian" in England and "Sumerian" on the Continent and in America. The invaders adopted the religion and culture of the Sumerians and consequently the Sumerian idioms began to be used extensively in the Semitic temples.[70]

If we consider all the Babylonian inscriptions of the period chronologically, we find that in the beginning of 4000 BC Semitic words crept into the Sumerian language until the latter language became almost Semetic. Again, the Sumerian inscriptions underwent a change ultimately assuming the Elamite character (another Tūrānian

---

70. *Encyclopaedia Britannica*, Vol. XXVI, pp. 75, 76.

language). In 3500 BC the language of inscriptions again became entirely Semitic. Thus it is clear that first of all the Sumerians and Akkadians lived in Babylon, and then the Semitic peoples of Arabia poured into the country, and after some time succeeded in establishing their rule there. The Semitic rule in Babylon is divided into two periods, the first dating approximately from 4000 BC and the second from 2400 BC. A brief history of these two periods, as narrated by W.R. Rogers, is given below:[71]

> *4000 BC.*—At about the beginning of the fourth millennium BC the Sumerian people, who had already attained *a high civilization*, found the land invaded by a vast horde of barbarians, for so these must have appeared to them. These were Semites, closely related in blood to the Arabs, who once overran Spain and the Hebrews, who once came pouring across the Jordon into Canaan. Whence these invaders came is not certain. It has been thought by some that they came from the north-east through the passes of the Kurdistān mountains, and that Babylonia was the land in which they had their first national development and from which they spread over western Asia to make great careers as Arabians, Canaanites and Aramaeans. This view, once stated and supported with suppressing learning, is now almost abandoned, but few great names may be cited among its adherents. A second view finds original home of the Semites in Africa either in the north-eastern or north-western part of the great continent. It were idle to deny that strong linguistic support for this view may be found in the recognized affinity between the Semitic languages and Egyptian, Coptic, Berber and the Kushite (Bisharee, Galla,

71. *History of Babylon and Assyria*, Vol. I, p. 452.

> Somali, etc.) languages. But when all has been said in favour of this view, there still remain more potent considerations in favour of a third view, that *the original home of the Semites was in Arabia, out of which they came in successive waves of migration to find larger and more bountiful lands in Babylonia, Mesopotamia, and even in the far western land of Canaan.* This latter view seems ever to find fresh supports in the newer facts, and to me it is clearly the best solution of the problems. It should, however, be admitted that it does not find the universal acceptance among the scholars.

Towards the close of the Sumerian period another Semitic race rose to power in 2400 BC, as the same author says:[72]

> The Sumerian civilization was old, and the seeds of death were in it. The Semitic civilization, on the other hand, was *instinct with* life and vigour. The Semite had come out of the free air of the desert of Arabia and had in his veins abounding life.

The following is the list[73] of the kings of the second Semitic period as ascertained from the inscriptions:

Name	King list (*years*)	Date list (*years*)
Samu-abu	15	14
Samula-ilu	35	36
Zabum	14	14
Apil-Sin	18	18
Sin-muballit	30	20
Hamurapi	55	43

72. *Ibid.*, p. 383.
73. *Ibid.*, p. 338.

Samsu-iluna	35	38
Abeshu	25	8(?)
Ammiditana	25	37
Ammizaduga	21	10 (unfinished)
Samsuditana	31	

Of the Arabian kings of Babylon of the second period Hamurapi is the most celebrated.[74] His predecessors could not gain reputation in the face of the growing strength of the Elamites, and hence royal titles are not found along with their names. It was Hamurapi who drove them out of Babylon and proclaimed himself king. The inscriptions of this House, available so far, belong to him alone. From one of them it appears that he was perhaps the first legislator of the world. Some of his laws have been found on a minaret of Babylon, which resemble the laws of the Old Testament.

The 'Ād in Egypt

Different evidences in support of the claim that the 'Ād ruled in Egypt also are given below.

The Arabs' evidence

Ibn Qutaybah writes:

> Among them (the Arabs) were the Amalekites (who were composed of different tribes) who spread over different

74. The Bible referring to the war between Iraq and Syria mentions the king of Shinar (Babylon) under the name of Amraphel (Gen. xiv. 1). As *Alif* and *Ha*, and *Ba*, *Pa* and *Fa* are interchangeable in Semitic languages, it is possible that "Amraphel" originally may have been "Amurali" the Hebrew form of "Hamurabi" (the suffix "il" meaning God is generally added to Hebrew words, *eg.*, Israel, Samuel, etc.). That Amraphel of the Bible and Hamurapi of Arabs belonged to the same country and the same period is by itself a strong evidence of their identity. Anyway, if this view is accepted, Hamurabi and Abraham should be taken as contemporaries.

countries and among them were kings of Egypt and Babylon.[75]

Ya'qūbī writes:

When the Egyptians made women their sovereigns, the Amalekite kings of Syria were tempted to conquer Egypt. So their king Walīd bin Duma' ravaged the country and the Egyptians had to acknowledge him as their ruler. He ruled in Egypt for a considerable time, and on his death was succeeded by another Amalekite king, known as Rayyān bin Walīd, who was a contemporary of Joseph.

We find in Yāqūt's *Mu'jam al-Buldān*:

It is said that the Pharaohs of Egypt were Amalekites and so were the Pharaoh of Abraham, the Pharaoh of Joseph and the Pharaoh of Moses.[76]

Ibn Khaldūn says:

Some of the Coptan kings asked for assistance from the Amalekite king of their time. He responded but occupied Egypt for himself.[77]

The Egyptians' evidence

Approximately in 200 BC, a foreign nation known among the Egyptians as Hyksos or Hycsos (shepherd-kings) occupied Egypt. Now, the question is: Who were these shepherd-kings?

The famous historian Manetho of Alexandria wrote a book on the history of Egypt in the Greek language in 260

75. *Kitāb al-Ma'ārif*, p. 10.
76. *Mu'jam al-Buldān*, Vol. I, p. 211.
77. *Kitāb al-'Ibar*, Vol. II.

BC. This book is not extant but some of its passages have been preserved by other writers including the Jewish historian Josephus. The view of Manetho on Hyksos, as quoted by Josephus, is given below:

> There were a king of ours, whose name was Timaens. Under him it came to pass, I know not how, that God was averse to us, and there came, after a surprising manner, men of ignoble birth out of the eastern parts, and had boldness enough to make expedition into our country, and with ease subdued it by force, yet without hazarding a battle with them. So when they had gotten those that governed us under their power, they afterwards burnt down our cities, and demolished the temples of gods, and used all the inhabitants after a most barbarous manner: nay, some they slew, and led their children and their wives into slavery. At length they made one of themselves king, whose name was Salatis; he also lived at Memphis, and made both the upper and lower regions pay tribute, and left garrisions at places that were most proper for them. He chiefly aimed to secure the eastern parts, as foreseeing that the Assyrians, who had then the greatest power, would be desirous of that kingdom and invade them.... When this man had reigned thirteen years, after him reigned another, whose name was Beon, for forty-four years; after him reigned another, called Apachnas, thirty-six years and seven months; after him Apolius reigned sixty-one years, and then Janias fifty years and one month; after all reigned Assis forty nine years and two months.... This whole nation was styled Hycsos, that is, Shepherd-kings; for the first syllable Hyc, according to the sacred dilect, denotes a king, as is Sos is Shepherd, but this according to the ordinary

dilect; and of these is compound Hycsos; but some say that these people were Arabians.[78]

The Biblical evidence

The first mention of Abraham in the Old Testament relates to his journey with his family from Iraq to Egypt. He referred to his wife Sarah (who was also his cousin) before Pharaoh as his sister, whereupon the latter desired to marry her. When Pharaoh knew the real state of affairs, he gave his daughter Hagar in his (Abraham's) marriage.[79]

After a century and a half Joseph went to Egypt. Though he was a Hebrew and the Egyptians generally hated the Hebrews and seldom mixed with them (Genesis, xliii. 32 and xlvi. 34), the Pharaoh of Egypt received Joseph with honour and appointed him as his minister (Genesis, xl. xli. xlii). The visit of Joseph's father and family to Egypt was celebrated by Pharaoh and members of the State with great splendour (Genesis, xlv. 16) and the death of Jacob was mourned and lamented by the Pharaoh (Genesis, l. 3, ii). It is noteworthy that Joseph advised the members of his

---

78. Josephus, Vol. II, p. 398.
A point to be noticed here is that the Arabs have given the conquerer of Egypt the name of "Shaddād" whereas the above-quoted historian Manetho has named him as "Salatis". Both the words really signify the same. The word "Shaddād" means strong and oppressive, so does the word Sallaṭ in the Semitic languages, from which Arabic words, "Sulṭān" and "Sulṭānah" have been derived.
The word Hyk may be taken as a corrupted form of the Arabic word *Shaykh* (meaning head of a tribe). The word "Sos" is decidedly Arabic, meaning management and supervision, from which is derived the Arabic word *Siyāsah* meaning administration. The name of the last king "Assis" corresponds to "'Azīz" in Arabic, a title which was till recently used for the chiefs of Egypt. The word "'Azīz" is used in the Qur'an also in connection with the story of Joseph.

79. That Hagar was the Pharaoh's daughter is not mentioned in the Old Testament, but in Jewish traditions.

family to describe themselves and their father as shepherds if the Pharaoh inquired them about their identity (Genesis, xlvi. 32).

From the above reference it is clear that the shepherd-kings have historical existence and that it was during their reign that Joseph and the Israelites domiciled in Egypt. The Arab historians also confirm this view. The fact that Joseph described himself and his family as shepherds, knowing that the Egyptians had great hatred for shepherds, shows that there was some connection between the royalties of Egypt and the Hebrews.

Some centuries after, the Israelites of Egypt were subjected to lots of hardships. When the Egyptians (the Hamites) succeeded in driving the Semitic rulers out of their country, they crushed the power of the Israelites (an offshoot of the Semites) who had risen into power during the Semitic rule.

> And the children of Israel were fruitful, and increased abundantly, and multiplied, and waxed exceeding mighty; and the land was filled with them. Now there arose up a new king over Egypt, which knew not Joseph. And he said unto his people. Behold the people of the children of Israel are more and mightier than we: Come on, let us deal wisely with them; lest they multiply, and it come to pass, that, when there falleth out any war, they join also unto our enemies, and fight against us, and so get them up out of the land. Therefore they did set over them taskmasters to afflict them with their burdens. (Exodus, i. 7-11)

Hence it is clear that the case of the Israelites in Egypt was entirely political. The Pharaoh referring to Moses and Aaron says, "The two magacians intend to expel you (people of the country) from your land" (Qur'an, 20:63).

Ya'qūbī writes in this connection:

> "Afterwards another king from among the Amalekites came to power. His name was Rayyān bin Walīd and it was during his time that Joseph went to Egypt. Then another king of the name Walīd bin Mūsā succeeded him and he was the Pharaoh of Moses."[80]

It is, however, an error to suppose that the Pharaoh of Moses was also an Amalekite, because the Amalekites had already left Egypt before Moses.

Manetho made a mistake in as much as he identified the Arabs with the Israelites. Being a foreigner he could not discern the points of similarity and dissimilarity between various offshoots of the same nation, as all Europeans are erroneously supposed to be Englishmen in India, all Muslims are regarded Turks in Europe, and "Arab" and "Muslim" are taken to be synonymous terms in Spain. Manetho says:

> That the kings of Thebasis and of the other parts of Egypt made an insurrection against the shepherds and that there a terrible and long war was made between them. That under a king, whose name was Alisphragmuthosis, the shepherds were subdued by him, and were indeed driven out of other parts of Egypt, but were shut up in a place that contained 10,000 acres.... That the shepherds built a wall round all this place, which was a large and strong wall... but that Thummosis the son of Alisphragmuthosis made an attempt to take them by force and by siege with four hundred and eighty thousand men to lie round about them, but that, upon his despair of taking the place by siege, they came to a composition with them, that they should leave Egypt,

80. Ya'qūbī, p. 211.

> and go without any harm done to them, whithersoever they would, and that, after this composition was made, they went away with their whole families, not fewer in number than two hundred and forty thousand, and took their journey from Egypt, through wilderness, for Syria; but that as they were in fear of the Assyrians, who had then the dominion over Asia, they built a city in that country which is now called Judia, and that large enough to contain these great numbers of men, and called it Jerusalem.[81]

Manetho here committed a number of mistakes. Firstly, the banishment of the Semites and the internment of the Israelites relate not to the same people (as Manetho describes) but two different peoples. Secondly, the Israelites were afraid of the Amalekites and not of the Assyrians. Thirdly, the Israelites undertook their journey by the sea and not by the desert.

It also transpires from the Old Testament that of the different Semitic peoples the Arabs were the most closely connected with the Egyptians. Hagar, mother of the Ishmaelite Arabs, belonged to Egypt (Genesis, xvi. 3). The wife of Ishmael was also an Egyptian lady (Genesis, xxi. 21). Arab caravans frequented Egypt,[82] and those who took Joseph to Egypt were also Arabs (Genesis, xxxvii. 29). When during the time of Joseph a great famine ravaged Egypt and neighbouring countries, the queen of Yemen (home of the 'Ād and the Amalekites) sent for corns from Egypt. This is confirmed by the inscription which the Muslim archaeologists discovered in Yemen in the first century of Muslim era.[83]

---

81. Josephus, Vol. IV, p. 339.
82 *Ibid.*, xxxvii. 26.
83 The inscription has been quoted in the introduction.

This inscription not only confirms the statement of the Old Testament regarding the outbreak of famine, but also throws light on the cordial relations between the Arabs of Yemen and those Arabs who were ruling in Egypt under the title of Hyksos.

Modern discoveries

What has been written by Manetho has been confirmed by modern Egyptialogists who agree that the Hyksos were Semitic rulers. Some go further and assert that the Egyptians themselves were descended from the Semites.[84]

The first and reliable evidence of the Hyksos being Arabs has been furnished by the German historian Heron who says:

> It appears that several tribes led incursions into Egypt from different directions, but those who advanced from the east, *i.e.*, Arabs, were most powerful, and pushed as far as Lower Egypt. ...Their long beards, long cloaks, and other things testify to their being Arabs.[85]

A German scholar, Brugsch Heinrich, who has compiled a book on the ancient history of Egypt on the basis of inscriptions, is definitely of the opinion that Hyksos were Semites, and that in the old Egyptian language the "Hyk" meant king and the "Sos" shepherd and the people of the desert.[86] The author has also quoted the view of the Arabs that Shaddād, son of 'Ād, invaded

---

84. Professor G. Rawlinson. *Ancient History of Egypt*, Vol. I, p. 981.

85. *Ibid.*, Vol. II, pp. 113, 118. Professor G. Rawlinson's (Vol. I. pp. 86, 111) view is that the weakness of Egypt due to its division into five kingdoms tempted the foreigners to attack the country from north-east, and the invaders known as Hyksos or shepherd-kings, who were Bedouins of Syria or Arabia, succeeded in capturing the lower province of Egypt.

86. Vol. I, pp. 273-274.

Egypt.[87] *A Guide to Egyptian Collections in the British Museum,* compiled in 1909, also endorses the view that the word "Hyksos" is compased of two Egyptian words "Hyks" and "Shasho" meaning the Shaykh or Head of the tribes of the desert.

In the modern period Rifā'ah Bek (an Egyptian) was the first Muslim scholar who realised that the Amalekites, the Semites and Hyksos were the same people. His history of Egypt entitled *Anwār al-Tawfīq al-Jalīl* was published in 1825 wherein we find the following passage:

> Their kingdom was named as the kingdom of the Hyksos and their kings were known in history as the shepherd kings. But among Muslim historians they were known as the Amalekites.[88]

Samuel Laing writes in this connection:

> There is considerable doubt who these invaders were who were known as Hyksos or Shepherd kings. They consisted, probably, mainly of Nomad tribes of Canaanites, Arabians and other Semitic races, but the Turanian Hittites seem to have been associated with them, and the leaders to have been Turanian, judging from the portrait-statues of two of the later kings of the Hyksos dynasty which have been recently discovered by Naville at Bubastis, and which are unmistakably Turanian and even Chinese in type.[89]

Various evidences in support of the Hyksos being Arabs are summed up as follows:

1. The Arabs' claim that they ruled in Egypt in ancient times.

87. Vol. I, p. 366.
88. Vol. I, p. 58.
89. S. Laing, pp. 29-30.

2. The Egyptians' admission that the Arabs entered Egypt as conquerors.
3. The correspondence in form as well as in sense between the name of the first Hyksos king and that of the conqueror of Egypt, as mentioned by the Arabs.
4. The Arabian or Semitic origin of the word "Hyksos".
5. The Arabian appearance and costume of the Hyksos kings as reflected in their statues.
6. The ancient relations between the Arabs and the Egyptians.
7. The similarity in manners between the Hyksos and the Arabs.
8. The references and evidences of the Old Testament.
9. The researches of the archaeological experts.
10. The testimony of Josephus and others and its acceptance by the European historians in general.

To the above may be added the following note of the ancient king of Egypt, Ramasis III, as found in an inscription: "I have crushed (the people of) Sā'īr who belonged to the Shashen tribes."

Sā'īr was a mountainous place in north Arabia where the Edomite Arabs had once established a kingdom. The mountain Sā'īr has been frequently mentioned in the Bible.

The 'Ād in other countries

The Semitic Arabs penetrated as far as Assyria, Persia, Phoenicia, Carthage, Crete and Greece. In 1200 BC the kingdom of Assyria was founded on the site of Babylon. Persia was not then a separate state, being only a part of

Assyria and Babylon. The Phoenicians, who were also known as the Aramites according to the Old Testament, lived on the Syrian coasts of the Mediterranean Sea. They were the first commercial people of the world who travelled from Asia to Europe, dispersing the darkness of barbarism and ignorance in which Europe had then been shrouded. On the one hand they sowed the seed of civilization in the barren land of Africa (Carthage) and, on the other, they illuminated the icy country of Europe (Greece) with their light of learning and culture.

We note below, brief though it be, the achievements of the Semitic Arabs in different countries.

Assyria

As said before, the Assyrians who were Semitic proceeded to Babylon from the Arabian coasts of the Persian Gulf, following the same route that their predecessors the 'Ād (or the first chain of the Semites) had followed. In fact the Assyrians were Arabs genealogically, and archaeological discoveries of Assyria also testify to it.

Persia

It is mentioned in ancient annals of Persia that after Jamshīd, an Arab named Ḍaḥḥāk ruled over Persia for a thousand years (*i.e.*, his dynasty).[90] Some of our historians say that Ḍaḥḥāk was the name of a Yemenite king,[91] but historically and archaeologically it has not been proved that the Yemenites ever invaded Persia directly. The fact is that the Arabs who had migrated from Yemen to the coasts of the Arabian Sea, and ultimately succeeded in establishing a kingdom in Assyria, invaded Persia and continued to

90. Firdawsī's *Shāhnāmah*.

91. Ṭabarī, *Tārīkh* (Egypt), Vol. I, p. 98.

rule there for a long time. The subjection of Persia to the Babylonian and Assyrian rule under the rise of the Medes in 600 BC, is now an established fact. Though the Assyrian period began in 1800 BC, its prosperity commenced in 1200 and terminated in 600 BC.

Phoenicia

The Phoenicians who had settled on the coasts of the Mediterranean Sea with Ṭā'ir as their headquarters, were masters of commerce from Asia to Europe. In Hebrew they are named "Aramites". The home of the Aramites was, according to the Arabs, in Arabia, and the Aramites also admit that they came to Arabia from Bahrain (a coastal town of Arabia) formerly known as Ṭā'ir. Archaeologically, it has been proved that in language, religion and customs the Phoenicians were Semitic, and consequently all the glorious deeds of the Phoenicians may be accredited to the Arabs.[92]

Carthage

The Phoenicians or Aramite Arabs settled in Carthage, a site where the city of Tunis now stands. The Arabs founded there a very formidable kingdom which terrified even the great Roman Empire. It was here that Hannibal rose and fought many battles with the Romans, and at last Carthage was levelled to the ground by the iron-handed Romans.

Greece and Crete

The first civilized country of Europe was Greece, and the Greek civilization and culture were wholly derived from the Phoenicians. This accounts for the fact that many commercial articles have got similar names in Arabic and Greek. The Arabs had a settlement in Greece and Crete also. The Greek

92. S. Laing, p. 7.

geographer Pliny says: "The Minaei, according to themselves, derive their origin from Minos, king of Crete."[93]

Strabo, another Greek writer, describes the establishment by Cadmus of an Arab colony in Euboea, an island off the coast of Boeotia, in Greece.[94]

The 'Ād as described in the Qur'an

From the foregoing pages it is clear that the 'Ād were a great people, founders of the oldest civilisation of the world. Asia and Africa were the centres of their activities and huge mansions and palatial buildings were the manifestations of their artsmanship. Naturally their rise and fall were eye-openers to the Arabs. Frequent references have been made to them in the Qur'an, some of which are given below:

> *Have you not seen how your Lord dealt with 'Ād, Iram, the possessors of lofty buildings the like of which were not created in other cities.*
> (Qur'an, 89:6-8)

Thus the Qur'an confirms the view that the 'Ād were descended from Aram son of Shem son of Noah.

> *Remember (O 'Ād) that God made you successors after the people of Noah.*
> (Qur'an, 7:69)

It is a well-known fact that after Noah the descendants of his son Shem (*i.e.*, the Semites) had established their kingdom in Arabia and its vicinity. It is, therefore, clear that the 'Ād and the Semites were the same people.

93. Foster, *Geography*, pp. 71, 75.

94. *Ibid.*

What is mightier in strength than we? [said the 'Ād].
(Qur'an, 41:15)

And my Lord will bring another people in your place [was the reply given to them by their prophet Hūd -Heber]
(Qur'an, 11:57)

Thus the Qur'an testifies to the greatness of the 'Ād.

Do you (O 'Ād) build on every height a monument: wain is it that you do. And you make strong fortress that perhaps you may abide.
(Qur'an, 26:128-129)

And (We destroyed) the 'Ād and Thamūd, and from their dwellings (this) is apparent to you indeed. (Qur'an, 29:38)

So they (the 'Ād) became such that naught could be seen except their dwellings.
(Qur'an, 46:25)

Thus the Qur'an bears testimony to the unprecedented architectural skill of the 'Ād. Yemen is generally described to have been the home of the 'Ād, but no definite place is fixed. The Qur'an, however, fixes it at Aḥqāf (sandy plains), as it says:

And remember the brother of 'Ād (Hūd) when he warned his people in Aḥqāf.[95]
(Qur'an, 46:21)

---

95. Aḥqāf is the well-known desert which lies on the south and north of Arabia, and hence there is no reason to confine the mission of Prophet Hūd to south Arabia only. The destruction of the 'Ād was caused by their social and moral degradation as had been the case with the Babylonians, Assyrians, Phoenicians, Carthagians, Greeks, Romans, and Persians. There has never been a change in the law of nature as the Qur'an says: "The same law of God was enforced among those who flourished before, and you will never find a

The prophethood of Hūd

Prophet Hūd was deputed by God to guide the 'Ād, as the Qur'an says:

> *And to 'Ād (We sent) their brother Hūd. He said: O my people; serve Allah, you have no god other than He; will you not then guard (against evil)? The chief of those who disbelieved from among his people said: Most surely we see you in folly and most surely we see you to be of the liars. He said: O my people! there is no folly in me, but I am an apostle of the Lord of the worlds: I deliver to you the message of my Lord and I am a faithful adviser to you: What! do you wonder that a reminder has come to you from your Lord through a man from among you that he might warn you? And remember when He made you successors after Noah's people and increased you in excellence in respect of make, therefore remember the benefits of Allah, that you may be successful. They said: Have you come to us that we may serve Allah alone and give up what our fathers used to serve? Then bring to us what you threaten us with, if you are of the truthful ones. He said: Indeed uncleanness and wrath from Lord have lighted upon you; what, do you dispute with me about names which you and your fathers have given? Allah has not sent any authority for them; wait then, I too with you will be of those who wait.* (Qur'an, 7:65-71)

---

change in the ways of God" (33:62). The law of God is that if any people are demoralized. He sends a reformer to them to lead them aright and warn them against the consequences of disobedience, as the Qur'an says: "We never punish a people until We send an apostle to them" (17:15). But when they do not obey their Lord, they perish.

Then as to 'Ād, they were unjustly proud in the land, and they said: Who is mightier in strength than we? Did they not see that Allah who created them was mightier than they in strength, and they denied Our communications. (Qur'an, 41:15)

And mention the brother of 'Ād, when he warned is people in the sandy plains, and indeed warners came before him and after him—saying: Serve none but Allah: surely I fear for you the chastisement of a grievous day. They said: Have you come to us to turn us away from our gods; then bring us what you threaten us with, if you are of the faithful ones. He said: The knowledge is only with Allah, and I deliver to you the message with which I am sent. I see you are a people who are ignorant. (Qur'an, 46:21-23)

And to 'Ād (We sent) their brother Hūd. He said: O my people! serve Allah, you have no God other than He; you are nothing but forgers (of lies). O my people! I do not ask of you any reward for it, my reward is only with Him who created me: do you not then understand? And, O my people, ask forgiveness of your Lord, then turn to, Him. He will send on you clouds pouring down on you abundance of rain and add strength to your strength, and do not turn back guilty. They said: O Hūd, you have not brought to us any clear argument and we are not going to desert our gods for your words, and we are not believers in you: We cannot say aught but that some of our gods have smitten you with evils. He said: Surely I call Allah to witness, and do you bear witness too, that I am clear of what you associate (with Allah). Besides Him, therefore, scheme against me all together; then give me no respite: Surely I rely on Allah, my Lord and your Lord. There is no living creature but He has it in His control. Surely my Lord is on the right path. But if you turn back, then indeed I have delivered to you the message with which I have been sent to you, and my Lord will bring another people in your place, and you cannot do Him any harm. Surely my Lord is the Preserver of all things. (Qur'an, 11:50-57)

'Ād gave the lie to the apostles. When their brother Hūd said to them: Will you not guard (against evil)? Surely I am a faithful apostle to you: Therefore guard against (the punishment of) Allah and obey me: And I do not ask you any reward for it; surely my reward is only with the Lord of the worlds: Do you build on every height a monument: vain is it that you do. And you make strong fortress that perhaps you may abide. And when you lay hands (on men) you lay hands (like) tyrants: So guard against (the punishment of) Allah and obey me. And be careful of (your duty to) Him Who has given you abundance of what you know. He has given you abundance of cattle and children, and gardens and fountains. Surely I fear for you the chastisement of a grievous day. They said: It is the same to us whether you admonish or are not one of the admonishers: This is naught but a custom of the ancients: And we are not going to be chastised. So they gave him the lie; then We destroyed them. Most surely there is a sign in this, but most of them do not believe. And most surely your Lord is the Mighty, the Merciful. (Qur'an, 26:123-140)

The causes of the decline and destruction of the 'Ād, as given in the above verses, fall under three heads:

1. Pride of Power

The 'Ād were proud of their power and said: "Who is mightier in strength than we?" (Qur'an, 41:15). Their prophet Hūd advised them to worship God, giving them hope that "God will substantially increase your power (if you obey Him)". But the 'Ād always turned deaf ears to their prophet, and so says the Qur'an:

> *Did they not see that Allah Who created them was mightier than they in strength.* (Qur'an, 41:15)
>
> *Fear God Who has bestowed on you all that you know—cattle, children, gardens and fountains.* (Qur'an, 26:132-134)

2. Oppression

The 'Ād generally oppressed and persecuted the peoples under their control, as mentioned in the verses of the Qur'an quoted above. Josephus also describes the high-handedness of the 'Ād, as he says:

> God was averse to us, and there came after a surprising manner, men of ignoble birth out of the eastern parts and had boldness enough to make an expedition into our country and with ease subdued it by force, yet without our hazarding a battle with them, so when they had gotten those that governed us under their power they afterwards burnt down our cities and demolished the temples.[96]

96. Josephus, Vol. IV, p. 338.

3. Disbelief in God

   The Qur'an says:

   > *And to 'Ād (We sent) their brother Hūd. He said: O my people! serve Allah. You have no god other than Him. Will you not then guard (against evil)?* (Qur'an, 7:65)

   Further Hūd said:

   > *But if you turn back, then indeed I have delivered to you the message with which I have been sent to you, and my Lord will bring another people in your place, and you cannot do Him any harm.* (Qur'an, 11:57)

   > *Surely, I fear for you the chastisement of a grievous day.* (Qur'an, 46:21)

At last the divine wrath befell the 'Ād, as the Qur'an says:

> *So We sent on them a furious wind in unlucky days, that We may make them taste the chastisement of abasement in this world's life; and certainly the chastisement of the hereafter is much more abasing.* (Qur'an, 41:16)

> *So when they saw it as a cloud appearing in the sky advancing towards their valleys, they said: This is a cloud which will give us rain. Nay, it is what you sought to hasten on, a blast of wind in which is a painful chastisement. Destroying everything by the command of its Lord; so they became such that naught could be seen except their dwellings.* (Qur'an, 46:24-25)

> *And as to 'Ād, they were destroyed by roaring, violent blast: Which He made to prevail against them for seven nights and eight days unintermittingly, so that you might have seen the people therein prostrate as if they were the trunks of hollow palms. Do you then see of them one remaining?* (Qur'an, 69:6-8)

Aḥqāf, also known as al-Rub 'al-Khālī, is a large desert extending over hundreds of miles. It is almost an impassable desert. Palgrave has described in his *Travels into Arabia* the chief features of the desert.

N.B

a. Prophet Hūd (Heber) has been described as father of all the Hebrews in the Old Testament. We do not find any evidence in support of this theory, but the Christian authors, however, favour this view. An inscription of 'Ād II discovered near Aden contains the name of Hūd. It is generally presumed that the tomb of Prophet Hūd is situated at the foot of a mountain of Ḥaḍramawt, which is visited by people up till now.

b. Many people suppose that the 'Ād were abnormally tall—possibly because they misunderstand the expression *Dhāt al-'Imād* (people of pillars) used in the Qur'an. The verse only means that they were great builders. The Qur'an says in another place: "He has given you (the 'Ād) physical superiority" (Qur'an, 7:69) (the word *basṭah* means power and strength).

   The same idiom has been used in the Qur'an in reference to Ṭālūt: "He has given him strength in learning and physique" (Qur'an, 2:247). None can logically infer thereby that Ṭālūt was very tall in size. The obvious meaning is that he was a very strong and stout man.

c. It is also supposed that after the Divine punishment none survived among the 'Ād. This mistaken view is based on the misconception of the following verses of the Qur'an:

So they (the 'Ād) became such that naught could be seen except their dwellings. (Qur'an, 46:25)

So that you might have seen the people therein prostrate as if they were the trunks of hallow palms. Do you then see of them one remaining? (Qur'an, 69:7-8)

But it is clear even to the meanest understanding that the above verses refer to the period when they were revealed to the Prophet Muḥammad (ṣ). As regards the survival of some members of the 'Ād, the Qur'an says:

So We delivered him and those with him by mercy from Us, and We cut off the last of those who rejected Our communications and were not believers. (Qur'an, 7:72)

And when Our commandment came, We delivered Hūd and those who believed with him by mercy from Us, and We delivered them from a severe chastisement. (Qur'an, 11:58)

And, indeed, He destroyed the 'Ād the First. (Qur'an, 53:50)

From the above verses it clearly follows that those of the 'Ād who were destroyed were known as "'Ād the First" and those who survived were called "'Ād the Second". Ibn Hishām Kalbī wrote a book on 'Ād the First and 'Ād the Second, but the book is not extant now.[97]

97. Ibn al-Nadīm, *Kitāb al-Fihrist.*

PART III

The Peoples of the Qur'an: The Arabs in their Own Country

12

Introduction

Now we come to those Arab tribes who stuck to their original home. Among these the Thamūd, whose reign began after the destruction of 'Ād I, were most reputed. Again, a section of the Arabs after having been defeated in foreign countries returned to Arabia and remained in power for nearly a century and a half.[98]

The well-known Arab tribes who either continued to live in Arabia or were forced back into Arabia by the foreigners are the following:

1. 'Ād the Second, who ruled from Ḥaḍramawt to Iraq on the coast of the Persian Gulf.
2. The Thamūd who ruled from Ḥijāz to the borders of Sinai.
3. The Jurhamites who lived in Ḥijāz.
4. The Ṭasm and Jadīs who governed in Yamāmah.
5. The Minaeans who were masters of Yemen.
6. The Liḥyānites who lived in al-'Ūlā in north Arabia.

98. Ibn Khaldūn, *Tārīkh*, Vol. II, p. 18.

Hamurapi's code

13

'Ād the Second

As said before, Prophet Hūd and all his followers were saved from the Divine punishment. It is mentioned in the annals of Arabia that he with all believers had migrated to Ḥijāz before the great Catastrophe occurred. Sometime later, among the descendants of these survivors a good king of the name of Luqmān came into prominence. He is said to have lived for several hundred years, like many other ancient kings of the world who are reported to have lived for an unusually long period of time. But in our opinion such a long period does not refer to the individual life of any particular king but to the collective period of all the kings of the same family. Hence we should mean by the reported long life of Luqmān the period over which the rule of his House extended.

Luqmān

It is mentioned in the annals of the Arabs that there was a sage known as Ḥakīm Luqmān to whom were ascribed a number of philosophical anecdotes and proverbs. Luqmān has been mentioned in the Qur'an, and some of his teachings are also referred to. We are disposed to identify the Luqmān of the

Arab annals with the Luqmān of the Qur'an, for which we have got a reliable historical evidence. The well-known historian Ibn Isḥāq (d. 151 CE), whose book on the life of the Prophet is the oldest work and who is taken as the first historian of ancient Arabia in the modern sense of the term, writes in his book *Kitāb al-Tijān*: "Wahab (the famous historian and narrator) says that when Shaddād, son of 'Ād, died, the government passed to his brother Luqmān, son of 'Ād. God gave him what He had not given any body else at that time, and endowed him with the intellect of one hundred men. He was the highest in size among his contemporaries... The son of Wahab says that Ibn 'Abbās told him that Luqmān son of 'Ād son of Mulṭāṭ son of Salk son of Wā'il son of Ḥimyar was a Prophet [the genealogy is not correct] without a revealed book."[99]

It is erroneously supposed by some people that Luqmān bin 'Ād and Luqmān the philosopher were two different persons. It is also wrong to assume that Luqmān the philosopher was African in origin who came to Arabia as a slave. Some scholars of Europe have identified Ḥakīm Luqmān with Aesop, the Greek philosopher, on the ground that the stories and maxims ascribed to them are of similar nature, but it has not been proved that the ancient Arabs knew anything of Greek philosophy. Moreover, if similarity in works necessitates the identity of their authors we shall have to deny the existence of a large number of historical personages.

A pre-Islamic poet of Arabia, Salmā bin Rabī'ah says:

> The vicissitudes of time have destroyed the tribe of Ṭasm, Dhājdūn, king of Yemen, the Peoples of Jāsh and Ma'rib and the tribe of Luqmān.

99. MS. Bankipur Library, Patna, p. 70.

These lines clearly show that Luqmān was an Arab, that he was head of a tribe in Yemen, and that he was once very powerful. All these qualities apply to Luqmān of 'Ād.

Luqmān's "Book of Wisdom" was frequently read by the Arabs. An inscription of the 'Ād which was discovered in 18 H contained the following passage:

> We are ruled over by kings who are aloof from mean thoughts and who deal harshly with the wicked. They guide us in accordance with the religion of Hūd, and all good decisions were embodied in a book.[100]

Luqmān, follower of the religion of Prophet Hūd, has been mentioned in the Qur'an:

> *And certainly We gave wisdom to Luqmān, be grateful to Allah. And whoever is grateful, he is only grateful for his own soul; and whoever is ungrateful, then surely Allah is Self-sufficient, Praised.*
>
> *And when Luqmān said to his son while he admonished him: O my son! do not associate aught with Allah; most surely polytheism is a grievous iniquity. O my son! surely if it is the very weight of the grain of a mustard-seed, even though it is in (the heart of) rock, or (high above) in the heaven or (deep down) in the earth, Allah will bring it (to light). Surely Allah is knower of subtilities, Aware.* (Qur'an. 31:12-13)
>
> *O my son! keep up prayer and enjoin the good and forbid the evil, and bear patiently that which befalls you: Surely this is one of the affairs earnestly enjoined. And do not turn your face away from people in contempt, nor go*

100. Ibn Hishām, *Tārīkh*.

> *about in the land exulting over much. Surely Allah does not love any self-conceited boaster. And pursue the right course in your going about and lower your voice: Surely the most hateful of voices is the braying of the asses.* (Qur'an. 31:16-19)

Archaeological evidence

Only one inscription of 'Ād the Second had been, so far, discovered in 1834 in the ruins of Ḥiṣn al-Ghurāb (situated near Aden). This was the first Arabian inscription discovered by the Europeans in the land of Arabia. The language and character of the inscription are in South Arabic, which is erroneously supposed by some people to be Ḥimyaritic. An English translation[101] of the inscription is given below:

1. We dwelt at ease for ages within the courts of this castle. A life without straits, and above wants.
2. Rolled in upon us the sea with brimming tide. Our rivers flowed with copious fall.
3. Among the lofty palms, their keeper sowed fresh dates, by the winding currents of the valley stream and also the dry.
4. And we hunted the game, by land, with ropes and reeds. And we drew forth the fishes from the depths of the sea.
5. And we walked proudly, in silks richly broidered with the needles. And in whole silks, and in green striped robes.

---

101. Forster's *Historical Geography of Arabia*, Vol. II, pp. 90-93. This is a poem of highest antiquity, found on the marbles amidst the ruins of a fortress, on the coast of Ḥaḍramawt, in the vicinity of the emporium of Aden.

6. Kings reigned over us, far removed from baseness. And vehement against the people of perfidy and fraud.

7. They sanctioned for us, from the religion of Hūd (Heber), right law. And we believed in miracles, the resurrection, and the resuscitation of the dead by the breath of God.

8. When enemies descended upon our soil to invade us. We went forth together, with straight and dusky spears.

9. Ardent and strenuous defenders of our children and our wives. On long-necked steeds, grey and dini-coloured, and bright bay.

10. Wounding those who fell upon us, and would do us violence, with our sounds, until they turned their backs.

The above inscription proves, firstly, that Hūd (Heber) is an historical personage; secondly, that the followers of Prophet Hūd were the only people of the 'Ād who survived the Divine punishment; thirdly, that the 'Ād were great builders; and, fourthly, that they possessed magnificent gardens, fountains, cattle, and a large number of children, as the Qur'an says: "*Fear (God) Who has bestowed on you all that you know—cattle, children, gardens and fountains*" (26:132-134).

The Greek historians and geographers describe 'Ād II as the people of the north-eastern part of Midian and name them as the "Oaditae". The Muslims were also aware of this residence of the 'Ād. But the general view of the Arabs is that Yemen was the home of the 'Ād, a fact which is testified to by Greek geographers also. Ptolemy makes mention of the

Adramitae and Adite among the tribes of South Arabia. We can take the first as 'Ād Iram and the second as the 'Ād. Ptolemy lived in the second century CE and hence the existence of the 'Ād up till that time must be taken as an established fact.[102]

J. Halevy and E. Glaser discovered a large number of inscriptions in the sandy regions of Yemen and Ḥaḍramawt, known as Aḥqāf. The place where so many inscriptions were found is now supposed to be the town of Ma'īn and the inscriptions are traced to the Minaeans. But as the place exactly coincides with the residence of 'Ād the Second, as the dates of these inscriptions go back to the sixteenth and seventeenth century before Christ according to well-known German scholars, it is not unlikely that the Minaeans were descended from 'Ād the Second.[103]

---

102. Aden which is situated on the borders of Yemen and Ḥaḍramawt may be taken to have been the headquarters of the 'Ād. In old times the general inclination of the Semites was to name a town after its founder. The towns of Arabia such as Raqīm, Saba, Ḥaḍramawt, Oman and Midian etc., were named after their founders. Hence we take Aden (ancient town of Yemen near which are situated all the buildings traced to the 'Ād and in whose vicinity the relics of the past glory of the 'Ād are still extant) as the abridged form of "'Adin". (There should be no objection to this form of plurality as the world "Banu" for plurality was used in north-Arabian language only). Forster ascribes Aden to 'Adnān, but 'Adnān whose home was in north Arabia had no connection with Aden Niebuhr, a European traveller of the eighteenth century, identified Aden with Dedan. He presumably loses sight of the verses of the Old Testament (Ezekiel, xxvii. 20-23), in which Aden and Dedan are mentioned as two different towns.

103. *Encyclopaedia of Islam*, "Arabs", Brill.

14
The Thamūd

After the 'Ād, the Thamūd rose to power, as the Qur'an says: "Remember (O Thamūd) that God made you successors of the 'Ād" (7:74).

As the 'Ād were masters of south-eastern Arabia extending from the coast of the Persian Gulf to the borders of Irāq, so were the Thamūd masters of north-western Arabia, then known as Wādī al-Qurā[104] (as their valley had in its fold a number of small villages scattered far and wide). The ruins of the valley were witnessed by Muslim geographers and some relics are still visible. The Qur'an has referred to this place as "Wādī" as it says: "The Thamūd who used to cut stones in the Wādī (for the purpose of buildings)" (Qur'an, 89:9). The town of Ḥijr, the headquarters of the Thamūd, was situated on the old road stretching from Ḥijāz to Syria. Another town, "Faj al-Nāqah," known among the Greeks as "Badneitu", also stood there. Now Ḥijr is called "Madā'in Ṣāliḥ", i.e the towns of Prophet Ṣāliḥ.

The history of the Thamūd is obscure. All we know is that they were a powerful people of north Arabia and like

104. Yāqūt, *Mu'jam*.

the 'Ād they were skilful builders. Their special profession was to erect houses, mansions and tombs of stones inside the mountains. The relics of these buildings are still available with inscriptions thereon in the Aramaic character. But most of these inscriptions belong to the Nabataeans who ruled in this place before and after Christ.

The period of the Thamūd began after the destruction of the 'Ād. The proof is that the Thamūd are more distinctly mentioned in Assyrian and Greek languages than the 'Ād, and the Qur'an also confirms this view when it says: "Remember (O Thamūd) that God made you successors of the 'Ād" (Qur'an, 7:74).

The period of the Thamūd came to a close before the advent of Moses, because the well-known tribes of north Arabia, on account of their political predominance, are mentioned in the Old Testament, but the name of Thamūd does not appear in the list; the Qur'an also supports this view as it says:

> *And he who believed said: O my people! surely I fear for you the like of what befell the Hordes, the like of what befell the people of Noah, 'Ād and Thamūd and those after them.* (Qur'an, 40:30-31)

The period of the Thamūd may be fixed from 1800 BC to 1600 BC. Another proof of the destruction of the Thamūd before Moses is that during Moses's time the people of Midian were found occupying the country which had been ruled over by the Thamūd. Those who have carefully studied the Exodus of the Old Testament will have no hesitation in admitting it.

Prophet Ṣāliḥ

When the Thamūd refused to believe in one God and began to worship the physical embodiments of stars, God deputed a messenger named Ṣāliḥ. In the Old Testament a son of Arphaxad has been named Ṣāliḥ, who is described as father of Abraham and Joktan. Christian priests who generally refer to the narrations of the Arabs and anecdotes of the Qur'an as unhistorical look forward to the Qur'an for sanction here, in as far as they say that "Ṣāliḥ" and "Salah" were the same person. If history permits it we have no objection. The Prophet of God invited the Thamūd to the laws of God, but they refused to listen. He then advised them saying, "*Here is a she-camel, which is a Divine proof of my prophethood. Let her graze on the earth. One day she will drink water and one day you will drink. If you have done her any harm, that day Divine wrath will befall you.*"[105] Good people believed in Ṣāliḥ and wicked people turned deaf ears to him. Nine men among the unbelievers entered into a conspiracy to attack Ṣāliḥ and his followers at night. They cut the knees of the camel and killed her. The anger of God befell them in the form of a serious earthquake. The Qur'an describes the whole event in detail:

> *And to the Thamūd (We sent) their brother Ṣāliḥ. He said: O my people! serve Allah; you have no God other than Him; clear proof indeed has come to you from your Lord; this is (as) Allah's she-camel for you a sign, therefore leave her alone to pasture on Allah's earth, and do not do her any harm, otherwise painful chastisement will overtake you. And remember when He made you successors of the 'Ād and settled you in the land—you make mansions on its plains and hew out houses in the mountains—remember therefore Allah's benefits and do not act corruptly in the land, making mischief. The chiefs of those who behaved proudly among his people*

105. Qur'an, 54:27-40.

said to those who were considered weak—those who believed from among them—Do you know that Ṣāliḥ is sent by his Lord? They said: Surely we are believers in what he has been sent with. Those who were haughty said: Surely we are deniers of what you believe in. So they slew the she-camel and revolted against their Lord's commandment, and they said: O Ṣāliḥ! bring us what you threatened us with, if you are one of the apostles. Then the earthquake overtook them, so they became motionless bodies in their abodes. Then he turned away from them and said: O my people! I did certainly deliver to you the message of my Lord, and I gave you good advice, but you do not love those who give good advice. (Qur'an, 7:73-79)

The Thamūd gave the lie to the apostles. When their brother Ṣāliḥ said to them: Will you not guard (against evil)? Surely I am a faithful apostle to you. Therefore guard against (the punishment of) Allah and obey me. And I do not ask you any reward for it: My reward is only with the Lord of the worlds. Will you be left secure in what is here: In gardens and fountains. And corn-fields and palm-trees having fine spadices? And you hew houses out of the mountains exultingly: Therefore guard against (the punishment of) Allah and obey me. And do not obey the bidding of the extravagant. Who make mischief in the land and do not act aright. They said: You are only of the deluded ones: You are naught but a mortal like ourselves. So bring a sign if you are one of the truthful. He said: This is a she-camel; she shall have her portion of water, and you have your portion of water in an appointed time: And do not touch her with evil, lest the chastisement of a grievous day should overtake you: But they stabbed her, then regretted. So the chastisement overtook them. Most surely there is a sign in this, but most of them do not believe. And most surely your Lord is the Mighty, the Merciful. (Qur'an, 26:141-159)

And certainly We sent to the Thamūd their brother Ṣāliḥ, saying: Serve Allah; and lo, they became two parties contending with each other. He said: O my people! why do you seek to hasten evil before good? Why do you not ask forgiveness of Allah so that you may be dealt with mercifully? They said: We have met with ill luck- on account of those with you. He said: The cause of your evil fortune is with Allah, nay, you are a people who are tried. And there were in the city nine persons who made mischief in the land and did not act aright. They said: Swear to each other by Allah that we will certainly make a sudden attack on him and his family by night, then we will say to his heir: We did not witness the destruction of his family, and we are most surely truthful. And they planned a plan, and We planned a plan while they perceived not. See, then, how was the end of their plan that We destroyed them and their people, all (of them). So those are their houses fallen down because they were unjust; most surely there is a sign in this for a people who know. And We delivered those who believed and who guarded (against evil). (Qur'an, 27:45-53)

As to the Thamūd: When it was said to them: Enjoy yourselves for a while: But they revolted against the commandment of their Lord, so the rumbling overtook them while they saw. So they were not able to rise up, nor could they defend themselves. (Qur'an, 51:43-45)

The Thamūd and the 'Ād called the striking calamity a lie.Then as to the Thamūd they were destroyed by an excessively severe punishment. (Qur'an, 69:4-5)

The Thamūd rejected the warning. So they said: What, a single mortal from among us! Shall we follow him? Most surely we shall in that case be in sure error and distress: Has the reminder been made to light upon him from among us? Nay, he is an insolent liar. To-morrow shall they know who is the liar, the insolvent one. Surely We are going to send the she-camel as a trial for them; therefore watch them and have patience. And inform them that the water is shared between them; every share of the water shall be attended. But they called their companion, so he took (the sword) and slew (her). How (great) was then My chastisement and My warning; Surely We sent upon them a single cry. So they were like the dry fragments of trees which the maker of an enclosure collects. (Qur'an, 54:23-31)

And that He did destroy the 'Ād of Old; And the Thamūd, so He spared not. (Qur'an, 53:50-51)

The Thamūd gave the lie (to the truth) in their inordinacy: When the most unfortunate of them broke forth with mischief. So Allah's apostle said to them: (Leave alone) Allah's she-camel, and (give) her (to) drink. But they called him a liar and slaughtered her; therefore their Lord crushed them for their sin and levelled them (with the ground). And He fears not its consequence. (Qur'an, 91:11-15)

And to the Thamūd (We sent) their brother Ṣāliḥ. He said: O my people! serve Allah, you have no god other than He; He brought you into being from the earth, and made you dwell in it, therefore ask forgiveness of Him, then turn to Him. Surely my Lord is Nigh, Answering. They said: O Ṣāliḥ! surely you were one amongst us in whom great expectations were placed before this: do you (now) forbid us from worshiping what our fathers worshipped? And as to that which you call us to most surely we are in disquieting doubt. He said: O my people! tell me if I have clear proof from my Lord and He has granted to me mercy from Himself, who will then help me against Allah if I disobey Him? Therefore you do not add to me other than loss: And, O my people, this will be (as) Allah's she-camel for you, a sign, therefore leave her to pasture of Allah's earth and do not touch her with evil, for then a near chastisement will overtake you. But they slew her, so he said: Enjoy yourselves in your abodes for three days, that is a promise not to be belied. (Qur'an, 11:61-65)

So far about those of the Thamūd who refused to believe in God and His Prophet. As regards the believers the Qur'an says: So when Our decree came to pass, We delivered Ṣāliḥ and those who believed with him by mercy from Us, and (We saved them) from the disgrace of that day. Surely your Lord is the Strong, the Mighty. And the rumbling overtook those who were unjust, so they became motionless bodies in their abodes. As though they had never dwelt in them: now surely did the Thamūd disbelieve in their Lord; now surely, away with the Thamūd. (Qur'an, 11:66-68)

And as to the Thamūd, We showed them the right way, but they chose error above guidance, so there overtook them the scourge of an abasing chastisement for what they earned. And We delivered those who believed and guarded (against evil).[106] (Qur'an, 41:17-18)

Thāmūd II

Thamūd II (*i.e.*, those of the Thamūd who survived the catastrophe) are met with in history in a more distinct way than 'Ād II.They are mentioned both in the Assyrian inscriptions and in the Roman history. The Romans, a little before Christ, had occupied Arabia Petra, close to the country of the Thamūd, and the predominant tribes of the vicinity at that time were Nabataeans and Edomites.

The Assyrian king Sarjon II who ruled from 722 to 705 BC, led an invasion into Arabia, which fact he alluded to in his inscription of victory. The subject races of Arabia mentioned in this inscription include the Thamūd,[107] which shows that

106. It is supposed that the camel with her young one was born of a rock of a mountain as a miracle of Prophet Ṣāliḥ in response to the demand of the unbelievers. The Qur'an does not mention it, though it has given a graphic description of the whole event. Hence we must reject it as a fiction. By carefully reading the verses of the Qur'an we come to the conclusion that the Thāmūd used to oppress animals and God sent a camel as His sign, saying that the day they oppressed her would be the day of Divine punishment. A certain hill of the Thāmūd is described as "Fajj al-Nāqah" by the Arabs and "Badneitu" by Ptolemy.

107. Hughes, *Dictionary of Islam*, p. 17.

they in their subsequent period could not obtain any power, and even if they did, they soon faded into obscurity.

Among the classical historians, Diodorus (d. 80 BC), Pliny (d. 79 BC) and Ptolemy (d. 140 BC) have mentioned the Thamūd.[108] The first has spelt the word as "Thamudani" while Ptolemy as Thamudiatae, but both of them have fixed their home exactly in the place specified by the Arabs.[109] Another Greek author Uranus (whose testimony is copied by Dr Sprenger) says that the Thamūd lived side by side with the Nabataeans.[110]

When the Romans occupied north Arabia, some members of the Thamūd were enrolled in the auxiliary force of the Roman army. History has it that during the reign of Justinian, 300 men of that tribe with long spears and camels were included in the Imperial army of Rome. As a large portion of their country had been occupied by the Midianites and the remaining portions were taken possession of by the Nabataeans, it is not unlikely that the Thamūd offered their services to the Romans in their invasion against the Nabataeans in order to feed fat the grudge they bore against them (the Nabataeans).

Curiously enough, no mention of the Thamūd is found in the Old Testament. The fact is that it traces the history of the world from its creation down to the days of the descendants of Abraham and then assumes silence from the Flight of Egypt (approximately in 1600 BC) up to the advent of Moses nearly 450 BC, and it was during this period that the Thamūd had their rise and fall. After this period the

---

108. Forster, Vol. II, p. 125.
109. *Goldmines of Midian*, p. 278.
110. Huart, *Histoire de Arabes*, p. 3.

Old Testament makes mention of only those foreign peoples who had diplomatic relations with the Israelites, and this advantage was not enjoyed by the Midianites, the successors of the Thamūd I (and hence no mention of the Thamūd I). When the Midianites were crushed by the Israelites in 1000 or 900 BC the Thamūd II regained some strength; and this was the period when the Assyrian king Sarjon II invaded north Arabia and obtained residuary from them (Thamūd II) in 700 BC. Afterwards, before the advent of Christ, the Nabataeans conquered the Thamūd II and when the Romans attacked the former, the latter sided with the Romans (and hence the mention of the Thamūd II in the Roman history).

Anyway, at the advent of Islam, no remains of the Thamūd were visible. Their land was occupied by the Jews and some minor tribes. Obviously, the Nabataeans might have crushed the Thamūd, as a punishment of the latter's unpatriotic activity in helping the Romans against their own countrymen. ❁

15

The Jurhamites

Historians differ as to the genealogy of Jurham. Some trace him to the first chain of the Semitic peoples, while others take him as descended from Joktan. Subsequent historians have sought to harmonise the two views by holding that there were two Jurhams—Jurham the First, and Jurham the Second. The former who was a contemporary of 'Ād was descended from the Semites of the first chain, and the latter who was a neighbour and relative of Ishmael was the son of Qaḥṭān or Joktan. He was the master of Ḥijāz while his brother Ya'rub son of Joktan occupied Yemen.[111] Anyhow, the Jurhamites

111. Joktan and his twelve sons are mentioned by names in the Bible, one of them, "Jerah" may be identical with Ya'rub of the Arabs. As the name of Jurham or any other name resembling that is not mentioned in the Old Testament, some scholars of Europe have tried to prove that Jerah and Jurham are identical. The confusion arises from the fact that the letter "ya" in Arabic and Hebrew and the letter "j" in Latin and Greek are interchangeable, and so in all European translations borrowed from Greek and Latin the word "Yarih" has been written as "Jerah" or "Jarih" which may easily be taken as Jurham. But it is a serious mistake. Firstly, because the names of persons and places occuring in the Old Testament were assimilated in Arabia through Hebrew and not through Greek and Latin, and it is not established that the letters "Jim" and "Ya" in Arabic and Hebrew are interchangeable. Secondly, if Jerah is taken as Jurham what will be the origin of Ya'rub? Thirdly, it is

settled in Ḥijāz as far back as 2200 BC, and Prophet Ishmael contracted matrimonial relations with them. An account of the Jurhamite kings has been given by Arab historians, which is given below:

> First of all Maḍāḍ, son of 'Amar Jurhamī, became king. A rival candidate named Sumida' waged war on him and was defeated. He then proceeded to Syria and there became king of the Amalekites. Maḍāḍ was succeeded by his son Ḥārith who was followed by his son 'Amar. Afterwards Mu'taṣim bin Ṭalīm, Ḥawās bin Jaḥash bin Maḍāḍ, 'Adād bin Ḍadād bin Jandal bin Maḍāḍ, Fatḥaṣ bin 'Adād and last of all Ḥārith became king. Ḥārith was the last Jurhamite king and it was during his reign that the whole Jurhamite tribe perished on account of their revolts and mischiefs.[112]

Arabs hold that Prophet Ishmael married in the family of Jurham,[113] but according to the Old Testament he married an Egyptian lady (Genesis, xxi. 21). This difference, however, is verbal rather than real. At that time the Semites (of the first chain) had been in possession of Egypt and had relations with Egyptians. It is, therefore, as correct to say that Prophet Ishmael married in the Jurham family of the Semitic race as to say that he married an Egyptian lady. The two statements are not contradictory as they outwardly appear.

---

impossible that two different pronunciations of the same name (Jerah) *i.e.*, Ya'rub and Jurham, obtained equal publicity in the same country and in the same language. Fourthly, when Jarham lived in Ḥijāz, the Qaḥṭānid Arabs had no political consciousness. Their importance began in 1000 BC after the destruction of the first and second chains of the Semitic peoples. We, therefore, favour the view of those historians who maintain that Jurham was descended from the first chain of the Semites.

112. Ya'qubī, *Tārīkh* (Europe), Vol. I, p. 254.

113. Bukhārī, *Kitāb al-Anbiyā'*.

The erection of Ka'bah by the Jurhamites and Ishmaelites has been referred to in pre-Islamic poetry of Arabia. A pre-Islamic Christian poet of Arabia named Zuhayr bin Salmā says: "I swear by the House around which people go and which was built by the Qurayshites and Jurhamites."

Pliny has mentioned a tribe of Arabia under the name of "Charmai" which may be a modified form of Jurham.[114]

At the advent of Islam the Jurhamites as a force ceased to exist, but some members were met with here and there. A certain Jurhamite of the name of 'Ubayd bin Sharīḥ lived at that time in Yemen. It is said that he embraced Islam in the presence of Prophet Muḥammad (ṣ). He lived up to the reign of Mu'āwiyah. As he excelled in the history of ancient nations, Mu'āwiyah got his verbal descriptions recorded.[115] In the third century of Hījrah, a historian Ibrāhīm bin Sulaymān Kūfī compiled a book entitled *Akhbār Jurhum* which throws much light on that tribe.[116]

114. Forster, *Historical Geography*, Vol. I, p. 124.

115. Ibn al-Nadīm, *al-Fihrist* (Leyden), p. 89.

116. Ṭūsī, *al-Fihrist* (Calcutta), p. 13.

Thamūdi dwellings carved into the cliffs at Madā'in Ṣāliḥ

16

The Ṭasm and Jadīs

The towns of Yamāmah, Bahrain and Oman situated on the Persian Gulf were inhabited in early times by the Ṭasm and Jadīs, who were descended from ʻĀd.[117] Political power was first in the hands of the Ṭasm, but a vicious and cruel king of that tribe named ʻAmlūk enraged the Jadīs by his misdeeds. When the latter (Jadīs) revolted, the former (Ṭasm) requisioned the help of the king of Yemen who responded but occupied the country for himself.[118] The Arab historians have named this king of Yemen "Tubbaʻ Hisān" but it is certainly wrong. Historians have been badly confused here as, on the one hand, they maintain that they (Jadīs and Ṭasm) were ancient tribes descended from Aram, flourishing between 3000 and 4000 BC, and, on the other, describe them as contemporaries of the kings of Yemen who lived only a century before Christ. The Greeks have mentioned an Arab tribe under the name

117. The original home of the Ṭasm and Jadīs was Yamāmah according to Kalbī, and Bahrain according to Ibn Khaldūn. The two views are not, however, contrary as, in old times, the two towns were known by the common name "Ḥijr" [Yāqūt, *Muʻjam* (Egypt)].

118. See *Aghānī* and other books on the history of Arabia.

of Jolistai, which perhaps stands for Jadīs. The destruction of the tribe Ṭasm became so proverbial that in the course of time the word Ṭasm in Arabic began to signify destruction. A pre-Islamic poet of Arabic, Salmā bin Rabī'ah writes: "The vicissitudes of time destroyed Ṭasm and afterwards Dhajdūn, king of Yemen, peoples of Jāsh and Ma'rib, and the tribes of Luqmān." This order shows that Ṭasm preceded the Sabaeans (people of Ma'rib) and 'Ād the Second (the tribe of Luqmān).

Yamāmah (formerly called "Jawa") is better known after its central town as Ḥijr or Qaryah. According to Hamdānī who was well versed in the ancient dialects of Arabia, the two words (Ḥijr and Qaryah) meant the same, *i.e.*, a town. In old Arabic the former (Ḥijr) was in vogue, and afterwards the latter, (Qaryah which is the exact translation of Ḥijr) took its place.[119] The relics of some ancient buildings in Yamāmah were visible during the Muslim period.[120] The Greek and Roman geographers have mentioned two Arab towns on the coast of the Persian Gulf or in Yemen, one under the name of "Gerra", "Gerrai" and "Gerrha"; and the other under the name of "Agraic". The Greeks and Romans in the course of their description of the Arab merchants have particularly mentioned the peoples of the above towns, as they had a prominent share in Indian trade.

These places were never seriously attacked by the Greeks or the Romans. Selucus, who had occupied Iraq after Alexander's death, led an excursion into Qaryah in 205 BC.[121] Anyhow, after the destruction of ancient tribes of Yamāmah and Bahrain, the whole territory became a deserted land,

119. Yāqūt, *Mu'jam*, Vol. VIII, p. 446.

120. For details of such ruins, *see* Yāqūt.

121. *Encyclopaedia Britannica*, Vol. XXIV, p. 604.

until the Ishmaelites and Qaḥṭānids proceeded there. Rabī'ah Ismā'īl, a clan of 'Anzah bin Asad, and some descendants of Qaḥṭān occupied Bahrain; and Banū Ḥanīfah took possession of Yamāmah.[122] When Islam came, Bahrain was in the hands of the Persians, and an Arab dynasty ruled over it on behalf of the Persian Emperors; Yamāmah still continued in the hands of Banū Ḥanīfah. Bahrain of her own accord accepted Islam during the lifetime of the Prophet. But Yamāmah once embracing Islam reverted and at last after a continuous war during the Caliphate of Abū Bakr was subjugated.

122. Abū Ḥanīfah, *Akhbār al-Ṭiwāl* (Egypt), pp. 17-18.

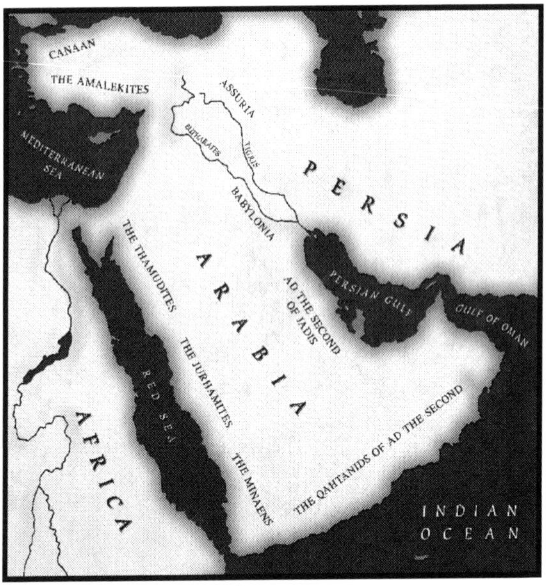

The 'Ād divided

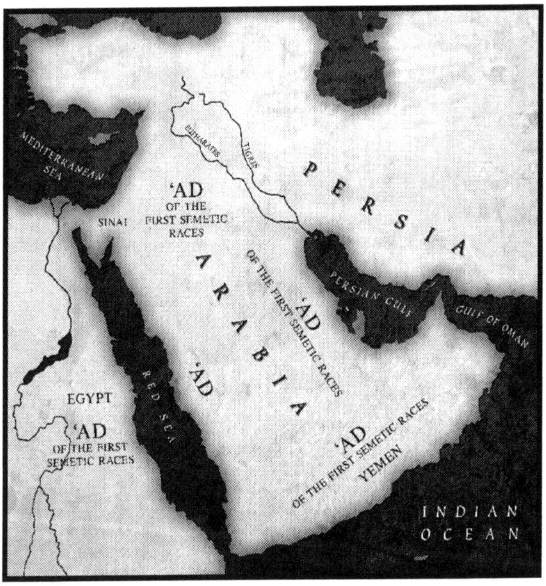

The 'Ād united

17
The Minaeans

The town Ma'īn was situated in Yemen with Ḥaḍramawt on its east and Saba (present Ṣan'ā) on its south-west. Modern archaeological experts, who have given pre-eminence to this town, have traced its ancient population, discovered many inscriptions and deciphered them with the aid of the Greek accounts. Modern discovery has fixed the location of Ma'īn in the site formerly occupied by the 'Ād II.[123]

The Minaeans are first of all mentioned in the eighth century BC (2 Chronicles, xxv. 1-7). Six centuries after, the Greek author Eratosthenes (276-196 BC) makes a passing reference to Ma'īn. In addition to him, Strabo (d. 49 CE), Pliny (d. 80 CE) and Ptolemy (d. 40 CE) have mentioned the town by the name "Mantai" and "Minaei" and asserted that it was situated near Ḥaḍramawt between Ma'rib and Qatāb (Katabania), with Charnaei as its headquarters. The Arab historians were also partially acquainted with the town, but they did not know the details. Hence the Greek

123. Ma'īn literally means stream in Arabic. In Hebrew the word is spelt as "Mi'yān". Another town of the name of "Ma'ān" exists in north Arabia at present.

account considerably adds to the knowledge of Arabs on the subject.

Now we give below the views of the Arabs and Greeks regarding Ma'īn together with the results of modern archaeological discoveries.

Arab view

Hamdānī writes in his books *Iklīl* and *Ṣifāt Jazīrat al-'Arab*: "The districts of Yemen, *i.e.*, Ma'īn and Brāqash (Yathil) are situated below the sandy desert of Raḥab. Ma'īn lies between the towns of Nishan and Dawb-Sharaqah." Yāqūt writes: "Ma'īn is the name of a fortress in Yemen. According to Azharī, Ma'īn is a town in Yemen, said to be located in Brāqash; and according to Aṣma'ī, Brāqash (Yathil) and Ma'īn are two fortresses in Yemen. Some kings of Yemen ordered the construction of the citadel of Salḥīn (Silee) which was completed in eighty years, and the fortresses of Brāqash and Ma'īn were built by the remnants of the materials of the above citadel. But, lo! there is no trace of Salḥīn now, but the two forts are still extant."[124]

From the above passages it is evident that Ma'īn and Brāqash were built by kings of Yemen, and that they were in existence till the second century of Hijrah. Brāqash is frequently referred to in Islamic literature as a town of some importance that continued to flourish down to the eighth century of Hijrah.[125] The two towns have been mentioned by Arab poets (for such verses reference may be made to Hamdānī's *Iklīl* and Yāqūt's *Mu'jam*).

124. Yāqūt, *Mu'jam*.

125. Khazrajī, *Tārīkh-al-Yaman* (Gibb Series, Vol. I, p. 100).

The above evidence conclusively proves that Ma'īn was the name of a town situated in the desert of Yemen, that it existed at least up to the close of the second century of Hijrah, that it was a seat of government at a certain period of time, and that a town named Brāqash (Yathil) was situated near Ma'īn. It is curious that these towns are described to have been built by the Sabaeans and Ḥimyarites. The Sabaeans being immediate successors of the Minaeans, the subsequent writers took them (the Sabaeans) as founders of the aforesaid towns.

Modern discoveries

The archaeological discoveries in Yemen are mainly indebted to two German scholars, E. Glaser and J. Halevy. They acquired several thousand inscriptions and deciphered them, which throw a flood of light on the religious, commercial and political events of that province. They also enlighten us on the extent of the kingdoms of Ḥaḍramawt, Qatāb (Katābania) Ma'rib and Saba, their seats of government, names of their kings, their religious ceremonies and practices, their modes of life and civilization, etc. Of all the kingdoms established in Yemen, that of Ma'īn has been traced to be the oldest.

Opinion is divided with regard to the date of the Minaeans' rule, as the inscriptions of the Ma'īn, available so far, do not contain dates. The German archaeologists are of opinion that the Minaean kingdom continued from 1400 BC to 700 BC. The French archaeologists and some English historians decidedly hold that this period began about 800 BC.[126]

The following appears in the *Encyclopaedia Britannica* (Vol. II: Arabs):

---

126. Clement Huart, *Histoire Des Arabes*, Tome I, p. 45.

> At the same time the facts that the inscriptions are undated until a late period, that few are historical in their contents and for the most part yield only names of gods and rulers and domestic and religious details, and that our collection is still very incomplete, have led to much serious disagreement among scholars as to the reconstruction of the history of Arabia in the pre-Christ centuries. All scholars are, however, agreed that the inscriptions reach as far back as the 19th century BC (some say, the 16th) and prove the existence of at least four civilized kingdoms of Ma'īn, of Saba, of Ḥaḍramawt and of Katabania.
>
> F. Hommel writes:[127]
>
> As early as the 3rd millennium BC the old Babylonian inscriptions mention a king Manium (also in the fuller form Manium-dannu) of Magan or East Arabia; there is much to be said for the view that Magan was only a Sumerian rendering of an Arabic "Ma'ān", and that from this centre was founded (at a date unknown to us) the South-Arabian kingdom of Ma'ān (later vocalisation Ma'īn) or the Minaean State which perhaps in the beginning embraced the whole of South Arabia (including Katabania and is mentioned as lying further off, probably covering Ḥaḍramawt). In addition a district named Melukh Central and North-West Arabia.

It must be added here that one of the ruling Arab tribes of Egypt (collectively known as Hyksos, Shepherd-Kings) is named by the Egyptians as "Main" which may be another form of Ma'īn. Moreover, the inscriptions of Ma'īn and Assyria indicate their mutual relations, and the Assyrian inscriptions whose period extends from 1900 to 700 BC make references

127. *Encyclopaedia of Islam*, Vol. I, "Arabs", p. 377.

to Maʿīn. For these reasons, as the French historian of Arabia Clement Huart says, the termination of the Minaean period cannot be fixed later than the seventh century BC.[128]

Another point to be noticed here is that the Sabaean rule in Yemen began approximately from 800 or 900 BC, and continued for centuries afterwards under the name of the Ḥimyarites. Obviously, therefore, the whole period of the Minaean rule or at least its period of prosperity must be taken to have ended before the ninth or eighth century BC. The fall of the Minaeans was followed by the rise of the Sabaeans. Some people take the Minaeans and Sabaeans as contemporary, but it is extremely unlikely that two powerful states could have continued in the small province of Yemen for centuries together. We, therefore, agree with the well-known German scholar F. Hommel[129] who has proved by facts and evidences that the whole period of the Minaean rule or at least its period of prosperity ended before the advent of the Sabaeans.

He writes:

> While it was regarded as obvious at an earlier period (*eg.*, by D.H. Müller of Vienna) that they (the Sabaeans and Minaeans) were contemporary, Edward Glaser, who is followed especially by Hugo Winckler and the writer of these lines, has championed, as is well known, the theory that the rule of the Minaean king preceded that of the Sabaean (and also that of the so-called Priest-kings), an hypothesis which would naturally pre-suppose a much earlier date for the Minaean (1200-700 BC at the latest). Lately, however, the hypothesis of contemporaneity has been again defended by

128. Huart, Tome I, p. 450.
129. *Encyclopaedia of Islam*, "Arabs".

> several scholars, particularly by the Arabist Martin Hartmann and the historian Edward Meyer; while Hartmann, it is true, now admits that the golden age of the Minaean kingdom preceded that of the Sabaean.[130]

Those scholars who consider the Minaeans and Sabaeans to be contemporary base their view on a Minaean inscription (Glaser No. 1155 and Halevy No. 535) which says that the Minaeans had their dealings in frankincense with Assur and 'Ibr-i-Nahrain and which refers to a war between "Madhi" and Egypt. By "Madhi" they mean the Medes who fought with the Egyptians in 525 BC. F. Hommel, however, holds that the term "Madhi" stands for the Midianites (or Manti, for by that name the Bedouins of Sinai were known). Moreover, in the above inscription Assur (Biblical mode of spelling) stands for Assyria, and 'Ibr-i-Nahrain for Algeria. Historically, the Assyrians lost their power in 700 BC, and the Minaean rule must be taken to have commenced long before that period. Consequently, the entire period of the Minaean rule must have preceded the Sabaean rule, or we may suppose that the first period of the Sabaeans coincided with the last period of the Minaeans.[131]

The Greek view

The Greeks and Arabs had only commercial relations. From the fourth century BC, Egypt had been in the hands of the Greeks and Alexandria was then the centre of trade. The Arabs were then masters of commerce in metals, incense and perfumes. Eratosthenes (d. 196 BC) writes on the tribes of Yemen:[132]

---

130. *Ibid.*, Vol. I, p. 378.

131. *Ibid.*

132. Duncker, *History of Antiquity*, Vol. I, p. 310.

> In the extreme end of Arabia next to the sea dwell the Manaean, whose metropolis is Karna; after these came the Sabaeans, whose metropolis is Mariaba; further to the west, as far as the corner of the Arabian gulf, are the Cattabani; whose kings dwell at Thamna; finally, the Chatramites are furthest to the east, and their city is Sabbatha. Each of these four districts is larger than the Delta of Egypt; they have rain in the summer, and rivers which lose themselves in the plains and lakes. Hence the land is so fertile that seed is sown twice in the year. The land of Cattabani supplies incense, the Chatramites produce myrrh; but elsewhere also fruits of every kind are plentiful and cattle abundant. From the Chatramites it is journey of forty days to Sabaeans; from the Minaeans the merchants go in seventy days to Aela (Elath). The cities of the Chatramites, Cattabani, Sabaeans and Minaeans are rich, and adorned with temples and royal places (Apud Strabon, p. 768ff).

From the above evidence of 200 BC it is evident that at that time there were four states in Yemen, one of which was Ma'īn, not less extensive than the lower Egypt. Its soil was very fertile and its chief town was Karna. It also appears that on the east of Yemen was Ḥaḍramawt, on the west, towards the Arabian Sea, was Qatāb (Katābania) and in the centre were Ma'īn and Saba; and that the distance between Ma'īn and the gulf of 'Aqabah (the route from Yemen to Syria and Egypt) was seventy days' journey. The following appears in *The Goldmines of Midian* (p. 179):

> Thence a straight line extends (northward) to the city called Petra and to Palaistena, whether the Gerrhaioi and Minaioi, and all the Arabs dwelling in the neighbourhood, bring from the upper country frankincense, it is said, and bundles of fragrant things.

According to Pliny, the chief products of Ma'īn were dates and grapes, but its real source of wealth was trade in animals.[133]

The Minaeans, who anyhow continued during the time of Pliny (d. 799 BC), had lost their power and glory in contrast with the Sabaeans, as it appears from the following:

> Pliny tells us that the Sabaeans were the most famous of the Arabians, owing to their frankincense, and their land reached from sea to sea. Their cities lay on the sea and in the interior, the chief city being Mariaba. One portion of the Sabaeans were called the Chatramites, and the chief city, Sabbatha, had sixty temples within its walls: further to the east were the Chattabani, whose city, Thamna, could enumerate sixty-five temples. The Minaeans lay in the interior beyond the Chatramites.[134]

From the above passage it follows that in the first century CE the Minaeans had been thrown into obscurity by the Sabaeans who were then the sole masters of the country from the Persian Gulf to the Red Sea, though the town of Ma'īn remained in existence up to the second century H. or eighth century CE. Pliny writes: "The Minaei, according to themselves, derive their origin from Minos, king of Crete."[135] This claim is probably the result of the Greeks' imagination. Nevertheless, it shows that the Minaean merchants had reached the borders of Greece also.

The area of the Minaean Kingdom

According to the Arab and Greek geographers, supported by modern archaeological discoveries, Ma'īn was situated in

133. Forster, *Historical Geography*, Vol, II, pp. 224-6.

134. Duncker, Vol. I, pp. 312-313.

135. *Ibid.*, Vol. II, p. 75.

the middle of Ḥaḍramawt and Saba (Ṣan'ā), in the southern part of Jauf.

> The Minaean Kingdom extended over the south Arabian Jauf, its chief cities being Karnan, Ma'in, and Yathil. Some twenty kings are known from the inscriptions to be related to one another. Their history must thus cover several centuries. As inscriptions in the Minaean language are found in al-'Ulā in north Arabia, it is probable that they had colonies.[136]

The Minaeans' colony in north Arabia (in the district of al-'Ulā) was not only a commercial station but a political town participating in war on behalf of its ruler. Samuel Laing, describing the extent of the Minaean kingdom writes:

> We are already acquainted with the names of thirty two Minaean kings, and as comparatively few inscriptions have yet been discovered, many more will doubtless be found. Among these known, however, are some which show that the authority of the Minaean kings were not confined to their original seat in the south, but extended over all Arabia and up to the frontiers of Syria and of Egypt. Three names of these kings have been found at Teima, the Tema of the Old Testament, on the road to Damascus and Sinai; and a votive tablet from southern Arabia is inscribed by its authors, "in gratitude to Attar (Istar or Astarte), for their rescue in the war between the ruler of the south and the ruler of the north, and in the conflict between Madhi and Egypt, and for their safe return to their own city of Quarnu." The authors of this inscription describe themselves as being under the Minaean king "Abi-yada Yathi", and being governors of Tsar and Ashur and the further bank of the river. Tsar is

136. *Encyclopaedia Britannica*, Vol. II, "Arabs".

> often mentioned in the Egyptian monuments as a frontier fortress on the Arabian side of what is now the Suez canal, while another inscription mentions Gaza, and shows that the authority of the Minaean ruler extended to Eden, and came into close contact with Palestine and surrounding tribes. Doubtless the protection of trade-routes was a main cause of this extension of fortified posts and wealthy cities over such a wide extent of territory.[137]

The Old Testament, describing the Israelite king Uzziah who fought against the Arabs and Philistines says: "And God helped him against the Philistines, and against the Arabians that dwelt in Gur-baal, and the Mehunims (*i.e.*, the Minaeans)" (2 Chronicles, xxvi. 7).

The war referred to above must have taken place in the northern parts of Ma'īn near Palestine. From this evidence which relates to 800 BC, the following conclusions may be deduced:

a. A colony of Ma'īn was situated in northern Arabia, as proved by archaeological researches.

b. 800 BC was not the date of the rise of Minaeans, as the French archaeologists hold, but was the date of the beginning of their decline, as the German scholars maintain; and hence their prosperity and glory must have dated much earlier than 800 BC.

c. The Minaeans were originally a political race, but during their declining stage became a commercial people. This is why we find that the Greek geographers from 200 BC to 200 CE, have mentioned them only as a commercial people.

137. S. Laing, *Human Origin*, p. 89.

The Minaean kings

The Arab and Greek historians have not mentioned the number and names of Minaean kings. We are indebted to the archaeological experts, who have, with the aid of inscriptions, enumerated twenty-two Minaean kings, as given below:[138]

1. Yatha'īl Ṣādiq, Waqah-il Yāthi', Iliyafa' Yāshir, Hifnum Riyām.
2. Iliyafa' Yāthi', Abīyada' Yāthi', Waqah-il-Riyām, Hifnum Ṣādiq, Iliyafa' Yātush.
3. Iliyafa' Waqah, Waqah-il Ṣādiq, Abīkarib Yāthi', Ammiyada' Nābit.
4. Iliyafa' Riyām, Hawfa'atht.
5. Abīyada', Khālīkarib Ṣādiq, Hifn Yāthi'.
6. Yatha'īl Riyām, Yubba' Karib.
7. Abīyada', Hifnum.

Samuel Laing[139] holds that the names of thirty-two kings have been found from inscriptions, and that many more are likely to be found when more inscriptions are discovered. Considering the long period of the Minaean rule, nearly 700 years, the number of kings stated by Samuel Laing is nearer the truth than the number given by Clement Huart.

If the Minaean period (of 700 years) is said to begin from 1700 BC which is the time of the destruction of the 'Ād, it must be taken to have ended in 1000 BC, which is exactly the time of the beginning and rise of Sabaeans (see The Old Testament's story of Solomon and Saba).

138. Huart, Tome I, p. 56.

139. S. Laing, p. 89.

E. Glaser and F. Hommel hold that the kingdom of Ma'īn existed prior to that of Saba, from about 1500 BC or earlier, until the Sabaeans came from their home in the north and conquered the Minaeans in the ninth century.[140] We have extended this period from the destruction of the 'Ād (in 1700 BC) to the rise of the Sabaeans (in 1000 BC) and thereby we get all the links in the ancient history of Yemen without much ado. Moreover, this view does not differ materially from the results of the archaeological discoveries. As the Minaeans' dialect and deities are different from those of the Sabaeans and resemble those of the Babylonians, it can safely be assumed that they were survivors of the early Semitic Arabs. ❁

140. *Encyclopaedia Britannica*, Vol, II, "Arabs".

18

The Liḥyānites

Arab historians including Ibn Khaldūn make mention of another tribe named Banū Liḥyān (the Liḥyānites), a clan of the Jurhamites.[141] Recently some inscriptions have been discovered in the town of al-'Ulā in north Arabia, together with Sabaean and Nabataean inscriptions from which we come to the conclusion that the Liḥyānites had settled in north Arabia on the Syrian borders, particularly in the vicinity of al-'Ulā. The Liḥyānite dialect not only resembles the Minaean dialect of the South Arabians but appears to have been derived from it. According to the archaeological experts, the Liḥyānites held power in north Arabia in the period between the decline of the Minaeans and Sabaeans (500 BC) and the rise of Nabataeans (300 BC). The Liḥyānite inscriptions are not clearly legible but this much is obvious that they relate to the period when Persia had diplomatic relations with Egypt (500 BC). It is not, therefore, unlikely that the Arabs, mentioned by Herodotus (d. 206 BC) in connection with the Persian invasion of Egypt, may refer to Banū Liḥyān, who lived on the borders of the said countries.

---

141. Ibn Khaldūn, *Tārīkh*. Vol. II.

The Banū Liḥyān lived between Persia and Egypt. Herodotus, describing the relation between the Arabs and Persians, says that the Arabs presented a large quantity of perfumeries to the Persian Emperor every year as a token of good faith, and not as a mark of subjugation or subordination, because the Arabs have never been conquered by any nation.

The following appears in the *Encyclopaedia of Islam*:

> The "King of Arabs" (Herod 3, 4) mentioned by Herodotus in 525 BC is very probably already a king of the Lihyanites whose capital Agar (Hagar), on the gulf of Akaba ['Aqabah] is mentioned by Pliny, and whose inscriptions, pointing both by their form and contents to the Persian period, were discovered by Euting in el-'Ola [al-'Ūlā], along with Minaean and Nabataen. Everything is in favour of the view that these Lihyanites were the successors in north-west Arabia of the Minaeo-Sabaeans and the predecessors or the Nabataeans, and that they are therefore to be placed about 500-300 BC.[142]

> The oldest are the Lihyan inscriptions, according to D.H. Müller... this is the oldest form of any south-Arabian script, and represents the connecting link between the old Semitic and the Sabaean script.... It is chiefly found in the district of el-'Ola.[143]

When Cambyses, the Persian Emperor, intended to attack Egypt in 525 BC, he had to seek the assistance of the Arabs (Banū Liḥyān). Herodotus writes in this connection:

> But as, at that time, water was not provided, Cambyses, by the advice of the Halicarnassian stranger, sent ambassadors

142. Vol. I, p. 379.
143. Vol. I, p. 392.

> to the Arabian, and requested a safe passage which he obtained, giving to and receiving from him pledges of faith. The Arabians observe pledges as religiously as any people, and they make them in the following manner: when any wish to pledge their faith, a third person standing between the two parties makes an incision with a sharp stone in the palm of the hand, near the longest fingers, of both the contractors; then taking some of the nap from the garment of each, he smears seven stones, placed between them, with the blood.... When therefore the Arabian had exchanged pledges with the ambassadors who came from Cambyses, he adopted the following contrivance: having filled camels' skins with water, he loaded them on all his living camels, and having done this he drove them to the said region and there awaited the army of Cambyses. This is the most credible of the accounts that are given.[144]

Pliny has mentioned a tribe under the name of "Liyānīn" living near the gulf of 'Aqabah. Some have identified them with "Liḥyānīn" (or Banū Liḥyān). But in our opinion they are 'Ilānīn (inhabitants of 'Aqabah) as the ancient name of 'Aqabah was 'Ilah and 'Ilānah. In the books of the Jews and Greeks the same name occurs, but at that time Banū Liḥyān were not in existence. "Banū Liḥyān" was also the name of another tribe of Arabia, descended from the Ishmaelites, who lived near Nejd at the time of the advent of Islam, and the Muslims had to fight with them once.[145]

---

144. H. Cary, *Herodotus*, Chap. III, paras 7-9.

145. In addition to the Semitic races mentioned above, there were many other tribes and clans in ancient Arabia. But most of them are obscure, and we know little or nothing about them. Nābighah, a famous pre-Islamic poet of Arabia, has enumerated them in one of his poems. Reference may be made to Ḥamzah Iṣfahānī's book on the subject.

Appendix

Appendix I: The Classical historians and geographers have mentioned the following towns of Arabia Felix (*vide* D.G. Hogarth, p. 18; Ptolemy's map of Arabia by Sprenger–Bevan, op. cit., p. 174):

Greek Names	Arabic Names	Remarks
Macoraba	Makkah, Rabba	Rabba means 'Great.'
Jathreppa	Yathrib	Pre-Islamic name of Madīnah.
Jambia	Yambū'	A town on the coast of Hijāz.
Dumatha	Duma	A town in north Arabia.
Egra	Ḥijr	Situated on the coast of the Red sea near Ḥijāz, ancient capital of the Thamūd.
Thaimai	Timāi	A town on the Syrian border of Ḥijāz.
Modiuna	Midian	A town of Joshua situated on the coast of the Red sea near Hijāz.
Sapphor	Zafār	An ancient town in Yemen.
Adana	Aden	A port of Yemen on the coast of the Indian ocean.
Mariaba	Ma'rib	Ancient capital of Yemen.
Minai	Ma'īn	An old town in Yemen.
Negrana	Najrān	A Christian town n Yemen.
Chatramoti	Haḍramawt	Situated on the coast near Yemen in south Arabia.
Gerrhai	Qaryah	A town in Yamāmah.
Catabaei	Qaṭāb	A city in old Yemen.
Nasao	Nashq	Ditto.
Karnaee	Qara	An old city in Yemen.
Sabaee	Saba	Ditto.
Maccala	Mukalla	A town on the coast of the Arabian sea, in south Yemen.
Omanun	Oman	The eastern province of Arabia on the coast of the Persian gulf.
Amithoscuta	Masqaṭ	Capital of Oman.

Appendix II: Genealogy of the Peoples of the Qur'an (according to the Old Testament) Genesis, i, xi., xxv.

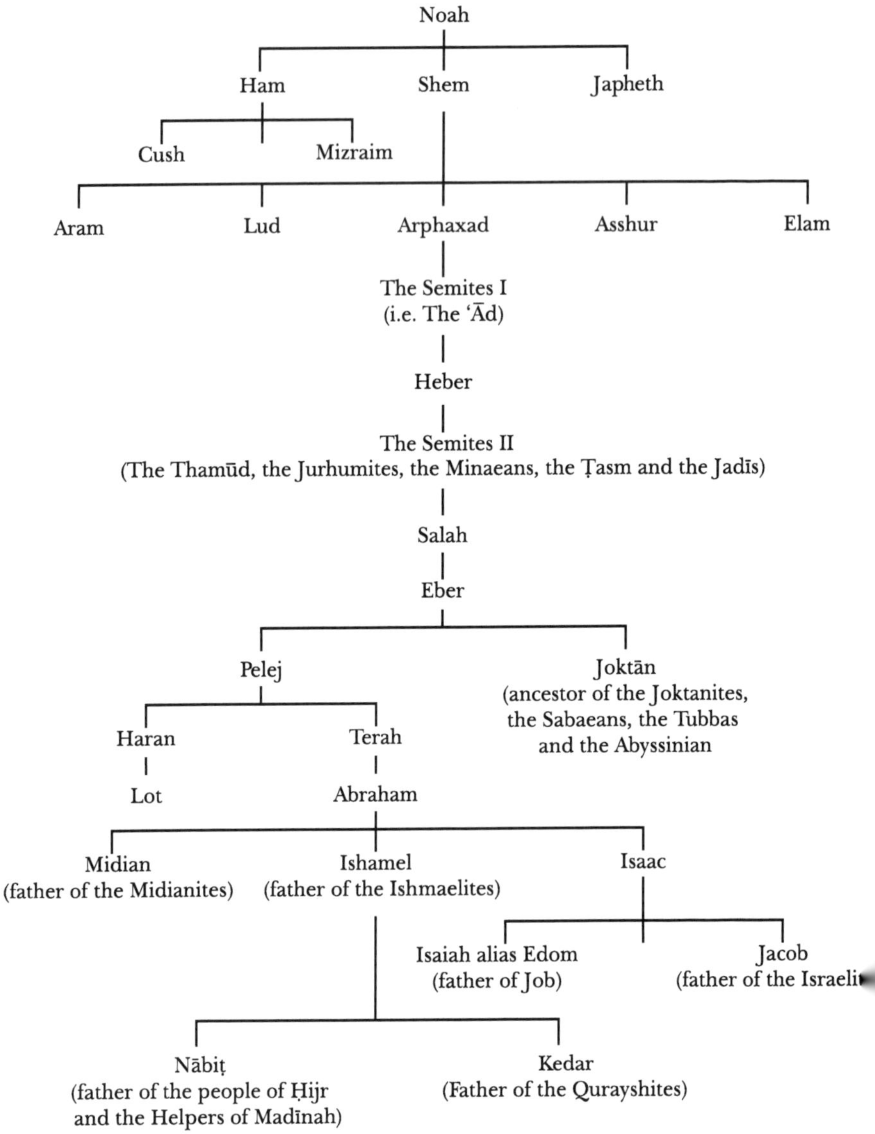

Bibliography

Works in oriental languages

--, *Ṣifāt al-Jazīrat al-'Arab.*
Abu al-Farj Iṣfahāni, *Kitāb-ul-Aghānī*
Abu al-Fidā', *Taqwim-ul-Buldān*
Abū Hanifah Dināwarī, *Akhbār-ut-Tiwali*
Bukhārī (Aḥmad bin Ismā'il), *Ṣaḥīḥ.*
Firdawsī, *Shāhnāmah.*
Ḥājī Khalīfah (Muṣṭafa bin 'Abdullah), *Kashf aẓ-Ẓunnūn.*
Hamzah Iṣfahānī, *Tārīkh-ul-Mulūk-ul Arḍ.*
Ibn Ha'ik Hamdānī, *Al-Iklīl.*
Ibn Hishām, *Tārīkh.*
Ibn Isḥāq, *Kitāb at-Tijān.*
Ibn Khaldūn, *Tārīkh.*
Ibn Nadīm (Muḥammad bin Isḥāq), *Kitāb al-Fihrist.*
Ibn Qutaybah, *Kitāb al-Ma'ārif*
Ibn Sa'd, *Ṭabaqāt al-Umam.*
Jurji Zaidān, *Al-'Arabu Qalb-ul-Islām.*
Khazrajī, *Tārīkh al-Yaman.*
Mas'ūdī, *Murūj-udh-Dhahab.*
Rifā'ah Bek Ṭaḥāwī, *Anwār-u-Tawfīq-il-Jalīl.*
Ṭabarī, *Tārīkh.*
Ṭal'at Ḥarb Bek, *Duwal al-'Arab wal-Islām.*
Ṭūsī, *Kitāb al-Fihrist.*

Ya'qūbī, *Kitāb al-Buldān.*
Yāqūt, *Mu'jam al-Buldān.*
Zakarīyah Qazwīnī, *Āthār al-Bilād.*

Works in western languages

--, *Around the Coasts of Arabia.*
--, *History of the Jewish War.*
--, *Philosophy of Jews.*
--, *The Empty Quarter.*
Amīn Rihani, *Arabian Peak and Desert.*
Bevan, *Ancient Geography.*
Burton, *The Goldmines of Arabia.*
Cary, H., *Herodotus.*
Christian Literary Society, *Arabia and Its Prophet.*
Duncker, *History of Antiquity.*
Encyclopedia of Islam.
Encyclopedia Britannica, 13th edition.
Forster, John, *Historical Geography of Arabia.*
Heeren, *Historical Researches.*
Hogart, D.G., *The Penetration of Arabia.*
Huart, C.L., *Histoire Des Arab.*
Josephus, *Antiquities of Jews.*
Laing, Samuel, *Human Origin.*
Philby, H. St. J.B., *Arabia of Wahhabis.*
Polgrave, *Travels into Arabia.*
Rawlinson, G., *History of Ancient Egypt.*
Rogers, W.R., *History of Babylon and Assur.*
Sprenger, *Ancient Geography of Arabia.*
Tazer, *History of Ancient Geography.*
Wright, W., *A Grammar of Semitic Languages.*

Index

I

J

K

Printed in Great Britain
by Amazon

74224687R00125